WHERE THE ACTION WAS

WOMEN WAR CORRESPONDENTS IN WORLD WAR II

PENNY COLMAN

CROWN PUBLISHERS ♕ NEW YORK

This book is for my mother—Maritza Leskovar Morgan, 1920–1997.
She taught me the importance of knowing history and the power
of words and images.

www.randomhouse.com/teens

Library of Congress Cataloging-in-Publication Data
Colman, Penny.
Where the action was : women war correspondents in World War II / by Penny Colman.
p.   cm.
Includes index.
ISBN 0-517-80075-6 (trade) — ISBN 0-517-80076-4 (lib. bdg.)
1. War correspondents—United States—Biography—Juvenile literature. 2. World War,
1939–1945—Women—Biography—Juvenile literature. 3. World War, 1939–1945—
Journalists—Biography—Juvenile literature. [1. War correspondents. 2. Journalists.
3. Women—Biography. 4. World War, 1939–1945.] I. Title.
D799.U6 C65 2002
070.4'333'08209044—dc21   2001028689

Printed in the United States of America
First Edition
February 2002
10 9 8 7 6 5 4 3 2 1

Contents

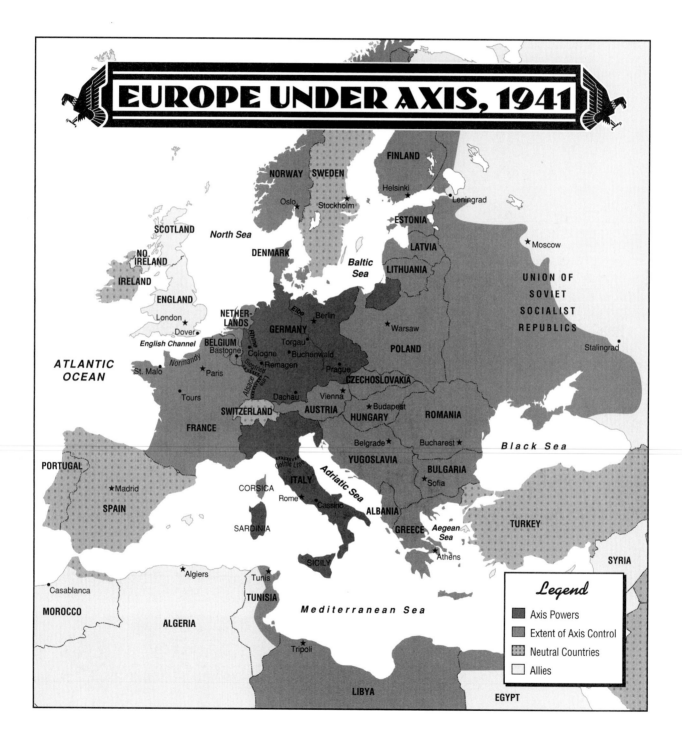

EUROPE UNDER AXIS, 1941

FINLAND

NORWAY SWEDEN

Helsinki

Oslo

Stockholm

Leningrad

ESTONIA

SCOTLAND   *North Sea*

LATVIA

Moscow

NO.
IRELAND

DENMARK

*Baltic
Sea*

LITHUANIA

IRELAND

UNION OF

SOVIET

ENGLAND

NETHER-
LANDS

Elbe

Berlin

SOCIALIST

London

GERMANY

Warsaw

REPUBLICS

Dover

Rhine

Torgau

POLAND

Stalingrad

English Channel

BELGIUM

Bastogne

Cologne

Buchenwald

ATLANTIC
OCEAN

Normandy

Remagen

St. Malo

Paris

Siegfried
Line

Prague

Alsace

CZECHOSLOVAKIA

Tours

Dachau

Vienna

SWITZERLAND

AUSTRIA

Budapest

FRANCE

HUNGARY

ROMANIA

Belgrade

Bucharest

Black Sea

YUGOSLAVIA

PORTUGAL

Gothic Line

BULGARIA

Adriatic Sea

Madrid

ITALY

Sofia

CORSICA

Rome

SPAIN

Cassino

ALBANIA

SARDINIA

GREECE

*Aegean
Sea*

TURKEY

SICILY

Athens

SYRIA

Algiers

Tunis

Casablanca

TUNISIA

Mediterranean Sea

MOROCCO

ALGERIA

Tripoli

Legend

■	Axis Powers
■	Extent of Axis Control
▦	Neutral Countries
□	Allies

LIBYA

EGYPT

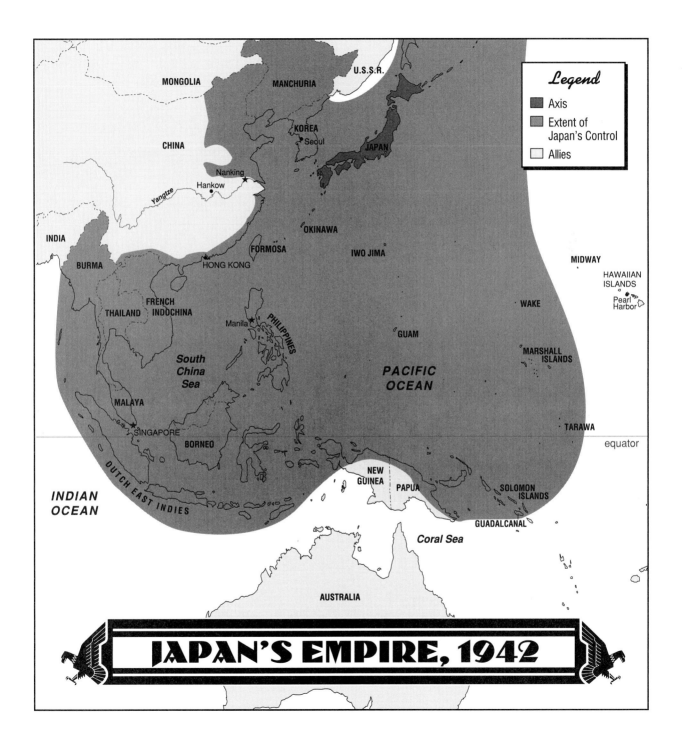

Legend

- Axis
- Extent of Japan's Control
- Allies

MONGOLIA

MANCHURIA

U.S.S.R.

CHINA

KOREA
Seoul

JAPAN

Nanking

Hankow

Yangtze

INDIA

OKINAWA

IWO JIMA

BURMA

FORMOSA

MIDWAY

HONG KONG

HAWAIIAN
ISLANDS

FRENCH
INDOCHINA

Pearl
Harbor

THAILAND

WAKE

Manila

PHILIPPINES

GUAM

South
China
Sea

MARSHALL
ISLANDS

PACIFIC
OCEAN

MALAYA

SINGAPORE

TARAWA

BORNEO

equator

INDIAN
OCEAN

DUTCH EAST INDIES

NEW
GUINEA

PAPUA

SOLOMON
ISLANDS

GUADALCANAL

Coral Sea

AUSTRALIA

JAPAN'S EMPIRE, 1942

Preface

SETTING THE STAGE

Today, in the twenty-first century, it is easy to take for granted the presence of women journalists. We see women reporting the news on television and hear them on the radio. Women's bylines appear in newspapers, in magazines, and on the Internet. No subject— business, politics, crime, disaster, science, sports, popular culture— is off-limits to women journalists. It has not always been that way. During America's past, men dominated journalism, especially in reporting war. But not totally. As early as the 1800s, against great odds, some women covered war.

Margaret Fuller reported the bloody Italian revolution of 1848. Jane Swisshelm wrote newspaper articles about conditions in Union military hospitals during the American Civil War. In 1898, Anna Benjamin went to Cuba and the Philippines to cover the Spanish-American War.

Mary Roberts Rinehart sailed to Europe in 1914 to cover World

War I. "I do not intend to let the biggest thing in my life go by without having been a part of it," explained Rinehart, who was thirty-eight years old and a popular writer of novels and magazine stories. Rinehart got closer to the action on the front than many male correspondents. "She was the envy of my jealous sex," one male journalist wrote. One night she got within two hundred yards of German lines. "The barbed wire barrier tears my clothes," she wrote in a magazine article. "The wind is howling fiercely.... No man's land lies flooded—full of dead bodies." As Rinehart made her way back to safety, she reported, "my heavy boots chafe my heel, and I limp. But I limp rapidly. I do not care to be shot in the back."

Where the Action Was: Women Correspondents in World War II is the true story of women correspondents who covered the biggest war in history. The record of their story is found in the countless numbers of their dispatches and photographs that appeared throughout the war in American newspapers and magazines, including the *Boston Globe, New York Herald Tribune, Chicago Daily News, Life, Collier's,* and *Vogue.* It is found in books that they wrote later and in their oral histories.

World War II was fought around the world in what the military called "theaters of war"—the European theater, the Pacific theater, and the China-Burma-India theater. After December 7, 1941, when the United States entered the war, 127 women managed to obtain official accreditation from the U.S. War Department as war correspondents. Although U.S. military policy prohibited women from covering combat, some women correspondents found a way to get to where the action was. They were determined that nothing was going to stop them from telling the whole story about war. That meant that along with the soldiers, they endured all the hardships

In 1916, Peggy Hull, a reporter for the Cleveland Plain Dealer, covered American military action along the Mexican border. (Left) She is pictured here wearing a borrowed uniform. Next she went to France to cover World War I, until she was forced to leave because the U.S. War Department refused to accredit women correspondents. After repeated attempts, she got accredited in 1918 to cover an American military operation in Siberia. (Right) Her "Correspondent's Pass" was the first issued to a woman by the War Department.

of war—they dug foxholes, wore mud-caked uniforms, bathed in their helmets, ate C and K rations, slept wherever they could, used primitive latrines, and experienced mortar barrages, artillery shellings, sniper fire, strafings, and bombings.

The story starts in the 1930s, with women correspondents who covered the military conflicts that led up to World War II. It continues through 1941, when the United States entered the war, to 1945 and the surrender of Germany and Japan. Women war correspondents were in every theater of war. Millions of Americans on the home front depended on their dispatches and photographs for news of the war and the fate of their friends and relatives who were fighting it. "They brought a fresh, new, and vital approach to coverage of the war," said John Oestreicher, foreign director of the International News Service. "And they did it without asking or receiving favors."

Nellie Bly, one of America's most famous investigative reporters, covered World War I for the New York Evening Journal. *Because the U.S. had not yet entered the war, she did not need U.S. accreditation. (Left) Bly interviewing an Austrian officer on the front. (Right) This article ran in the December 14, 1914, edition.*

Famous Writer in Austria for the Journal

NELLIE BLY ON THE FIRING LINE

The following is the first of the articles to come from Miss Nellie Bly, special correspondent for the Evening Journal, who is now at the front in the beleaguered fortress of Przemysl in Austria:

Przemysl, Friday, Oct. 30, 1914.
—I went on the firing line yesterday. It was Thursday, October 29, 1914. I was called at 5 o'clock. I made my unsatisfactory toilet in the dark. My electric light had gone to sleep and the daylight was not yet on duty.

At six I walked down four long flights of stairs—dirty stairs—pushing through a crowd of soldiers who were raising a frightful and unsanitary dust by brushing and polishing officers' uniforms and boots.

I walked one' block to the coffee house—Cafe Stelber. Three miniature waiters—they all loc: like dwarfs in this country—in the same dirty clothes they have worn since my arrival, stood talking to the girl behind the counter. All tables were smeared with ashes of the night's smokers, so I resignedly sat down. There was no choice.

But I think they would be clean if they were taught and knew the importance of cleanliness. It is one thing, perhaps the first, this war will teach them—the importance of sanitary cleanliness.

BREAKFAST FOR 15 CENTS.

A smiling, pleasant woman with a bucket of cold, dirty water, a dirtier rag and no soap, came rushing to wipe my table and the floor under

Nellie Bly

humanity. The first and most important thing for Austria is an able, efficient sanitary commander and corps with power.

A matter of four weeks ago the village of Hermanowice occupied the bank on the other side of the small stream, which separates it from the camp. A few chimneys still stand. Piles of brick, plaster and logs show where homes once stood. Gardens trampled out yet green, with touches of blooming poppies and ginger, have not perished under the feet of the thousands of Russians, who, after capturing this place, slowly retreated three weeks ago with enormous losses. On the branches of felled trees soldiers hung their clothes, which they washed in the stream and their unwashed coats and blankets.

The field kitchens were busy. They are like a square steel tank, riveted and set on four wheels. Underneath is a place for wood, the small door located between the hind wheels. On top are the holes in which are fitted three enormous pots, shaped like a range boiler. Each pot has a heavy steel cover, which locks when turned. At the back hang two heavy steel dippers stamped with the coat of arms of Austria.

Each field kitchen cooks for 250 men at one time. Once every five days each man gets 3½ kilos of bread and 200 grams of biscuit. In the morning he gets coffee or tea. In the middle of the day he gets meat stewed, vegetables and sometimes rice.

"What does he have for supper?" I asked Colonel John.

"Oh, for supper he does not get much," he replied, "only black bread and coffee."

The cook was chopping meat into shreds on a board supported by two iron braces on the side of the kitchen. He chopped or shredded the meat very fine and dropped the bits into the pots.

The meat looked and smelt fresh. It had been killed two days before. On upright poles soldiers were weaving straw mats for wagon covers. From one camp rang the blacksmith's anvil. I was glad when we left the camps and in our unique wagons joined the winding trails on the

A series of articles on the war by the celebrated newspaper woman, Nellie Bly, will appear in the Evening Journal from time to time. Miss Bly

Chapter 1

PRELUDE TO WORLD WAR II
IN EUROPE

With a knapsack and fifty dollars, Martha Gellhorn traveled to
Spain to cover her first war, the Spanish civil war. Confident and
fearless, Gellhorn was a foreign correspondent for *Collier's*, a
popular weekly magazine. She was twenty-nine years old, and
she would spend the next fifty-three years of her life covering
wars. When she died in 1998, the *London Daily Telegraph* honored
her as "one of the great war correspondents of the century—
brave, fierce and wholly committed to the truth of the situation."

Martha Gellhorn grew up in St. Louis, Missouri. From an early
age she attended protest marches with her mother, a tireless
activist, and she decided that her "plan for life was to go every-
where, see everything, and write about it."

The Spanish civil war began in 1936, when Generalissimo
Francisco Franco led a revolt against the legally elected government of Spain. Arriving in 1937, Martha Gellhorn toured war-torn

Spain by car, on horseback, and on foot. During her time at the front lines, she learned how to identify types of weapons from their sounds and "to gauge shell burst and know what is dangerous and what is not."

During the siege of Madrid, Gellhorn stayed at the Hotel Florida, where she could walk to the front lines, just ten or fifteen blocks away. One day a shell hit the hotel.

Martha Gellhorn at the front during the Spanish civil war.

Creating a word picture of sights, sounds, and feelings, Martha Gellhorn described the scene: "Suddenly there came that whistle-whine-scream-roar and the noise was in your throat and you couldn't feel or hear or think and the building shook and seemed to settle. Outside in the hall, the maids were calling to one another like birds, in high excited voices. On the floor above...there was nothing left in that room, the furniture was kindling wood, the walls were stripped and in places torn open, a great hole led into the next room and the bed was twisted iron and stood upright and silly against the wall."

Gellhorn noticed that the male war correspondents stayed away from hospitals with wounded civilians and soldiers. She, however, did not. "I was a great frequenter of hospitals," she explained, "because that's where you see what war really costs." Throughout her career, she wrote many graphic descriptions of the devastating impact of war on everything it touched—the landscape, buildings, animals, men, women, and children. "I always thought that if I could make anyone who had not seen such suffering begin to imagine the suffering, they would insist on a world which refused to allow such suffering," she wrote.

Martha Gellhorn was not the only American woman correspondent who went to Spain. Virginia Cowles, a correspondent for the Hearst newspapers who was fluent in French and Italian, covered the war in high heels, and became good friends with Martha Gellhorn. "I had no qualifications as a war correspondent except curiosity," Cowles later explained. "Although I had traveled in Europe and the Far East a good deal, and written a number of articles...my adventures were of a peaceful nature.... When the war broke out in Spain, I saw an opportunity for more vigorous reporting."

Martha Gellhorn and other correspondents were particularly drawn to the Spanish civil war because of the other countries involved in the conflict. Joseph Stalin, leader of the Communist Soviet Union, was sending small amounts of aid to the forces that were fighting to save the government. Adolf Hitler, leader of Nazi Germany, and Benito Mussolini, leader of Fascist Italy, were providing soldiers, supplies, and planes to Generalissimo Franco's forces.

By the time Gellhorn arrived, Italy had also invaded and conquered Ethiopia in Africa. Sonia Tomara, a correspondent for the *New York Herald Tribune*, covered that story.

The daughter of Russian aristocrats, Tomara was a teenager when the Russian revolution began in 1917. She witnessed fierce fighting and hardship. Once, she and her younger sister got caught in the middle of a battle and were captured; they were accused of

Eleanor Packard, a correspondent for the United Press, boarding an Italian observation plane in 1936 during Italy's invasion of Ethiopia.

Margaret Bourke-White, a famous American photographer, shot this crowd of forty thousand Sudeten Germans giving the Nazi salute at a rally in Czechoslovakia in 1938.

spying and sentenced to be executed the next day. "I sat alone in a cell all that afternoon," Tomara later recalled, "trying to imagine how I would behave on the way to death." The sisters were spared when a sympathetic guard helped them escape.

Fluent in many languages and a skilled writer, Tomara supported her family, who had fled to Paris, as a newspaper correspondent. In 1936, she broke the story of the Rome-Berlin Axis, an alliance between Mussolini and Hitler.

That same year, Hitler's troops had reoccupied the Rhineland, an industrial area that Germany had lost to France in World War I. Two years later, Hitler's troops marched into Austria. A few months after that, he threatened to take over Czechoslovakia.

Margaret Bourke-White, a famous photographer for *Life*, was in Czechoslovakia during that tense time. A dynamic, daring woman, Bourke-White was a pioneer in photojournalism, stories told through photographs. Crisscrossing Czechoslovakia, she photographed schoolgirls, fieldworkers, Gypsies, and a Nazi storm troopers' training class for little boys who were Sudeten Germans (Germans who lived in Czechoslovakia).

Martha Gellhorn also went to Czechoslovakia, reporting that "they talk a great deal about democracy in Czechoslovakia because they think they may have to fight for it." With their well-equipped army and the belief that Great Britain and France would help them, the Czechs were optimistic, Gellhorn wrote. In her article, she quoted the words of a popular Czech song: "All right, Adolf, come ahead."

The optimism ended in the autumn of 1938, when the leaders of Great Britain and France agreed to let Hitler take part of Czechoslovakia. Six months later, his troops occupied the whole country.

Virginia Cowles covered the takeover of Czechoslovakia for the London *Sunday Times*. At one point, she and two male reporters were arrested and held for hours by a Sudeten German guard with a machine gun. "We were so afraid that a move would upset him," she wrote, "we scarcely dared to turn our heads."

Margaret Bourke-White's precarious perch on an eagle gargoyle outside her photo studio on the sixty-first floor of the Chrysler Building in New York City.

Finally, after convincing authorities that they were foreign correspondents, Cowles and her colleagues were released.

Before Cowles left Czechoslovakia, she went to Carlsbad to hear Hitler speak. "It was a grey rainy day...," she wrote, and "the town was already overflowing with German troops and S.S. [*Schutzstaffel*, Hitler's elite guard] men. Hundreds of workmen were erecting triumphal arches across the streets—huge wreaths of flowers entwined which spelt the words '*Wir danken unseren Führer* (We thank our Leader).'"

Cowles noted that Hitler's speech was short and without much conviction, except for the moment he raised his voice, hit the microphone, and declared, "That I would be standing here one day, I knew."

The New York Times.

"All the News That's Fit to Print."

EXTRA

VOL. LXXXVIII...No. 29,805.

NEW YORK, FRIDAY, SEPTEMBER 1, 1939.

THREE CENTS

*GERMAN ARMY ATTACKS POLAND;
CITIES BOMBED, PORT BLOCKADED;
DANZIG IS ACCEPTED INTO REICH*

Chapter 2

SOUNDING THE ALARM IN EUROPE

Throughout the 1930s, women foreign correspondents had been sounding the alarm about Hitler. Sigrid Schultz, according to a male correspondent, was "Adolf Hitler's greatest enemy." An American by birth, Schultz had grown up in Europe. Fluent in several languages, she got a job as an interpreter at the *Chicago Tribune*'s news bureau in Berlin, Germany. She quickly proved her ability to report a news story, and in 1925, she was made head of the news bureau.

Schultz boldly reported how Hitler and his political party, the National Socialist German Workers' Party, or the Nazi Party, systematically took control of the government, newspapers, radio stations, factories, businesses, labor unions, courts, and schools. How hundreds of anti-Semitic laws were passed—four hundred by 1938. How Jews were fired from their jobs, forced to quit being doctors and lawyers, ordered to leave school. How anyone who

"Adolf Hitler's greatest enemy"—Sigrid Schultz in Berlin in 1928.

opposed Hitler was exiled, beaten up, or executed. How the first concentration camp was built at Dachau in 1933. How Germany was building up its military force.

And Sigrid Schultz reported all this right from Berlin, the capital of Nazi Germany. When it became too dangerous for her to publish articles under her byline, she used the pseudonym John Dickson.

In 1939, Schultz heard gossip that Hitler regularly consulted with an astrologer. She visited the astrologer and learned that Hitler was considering an alliance with the Soviet Union. Since Hitler had consistently denounced the Russians, this was startling news. Schultz checked and double-checked her sources. Finally, convinced that the information was true, she reported in a radio broadcast and a newspaper article that "the newest toast in high Hitler-Guard circles is: To our new ally, Russia."

Her scoop was soon confirmed when Germany and the Soviet

Union announced that they had signed a mutual nonaggression pact. Now the Russians would remain neutral if Germany went to war. They also secretly agreed to divide Poland, a country that lay between Germany and Russia.

On September 1, 1939, German troops, tanks, and planes invaded Poland from the west. Virginia Cowles arrived in Berlin seventeen hours before Hitler gave the order to attack. "You knew the machine was ready," she wrote. "The planes and tanks were waiting and the guns were in position. Everything was ready down to the polish on the last button of the last uniform."

Great Britain and France warned Hitler that they would go to war if he did not withdraw his troops. Hitler ignored them. On September 3, Great Britain and France, known as the Allies, declared war on Germany, officially starting World War II.

On September 17, Russian troops marched into Poland across the eastern border. "Poland's two powerful neighbors were squeezing in on her like a giant nutcracker," wrote Virginia Cowles, who went to cover what she described as the "Polish massacre."

Sonia Tomara was in Warsaw, the capital of Poland, when the war began. Although she could not file dispatches about the air raids and frantic refugees because the Germans had destroyed the telephone and telegraph lines, Tomara did make a radio broadcast to the United States. Finally, the Germans circled Warsaw on three sides, and the Polish government fled. Tomara left in a car with three male correspondents. She took only a few belongings, a gas mask, and her camera and typewriter.

After Germany and Russia divided Poland, the war seemed to stop. Neither side launched a major attack. Some people began saying it was "a phony war," but not Martha Gellhorn. "I thought it would be a hell-on-earth war and a long one," she later wrote.

In November 1939, Gellhorn's editor at *Collier's* sent her to Finland because he thought something was about to happen there. She spent two weeks on a ship that slowly made its way through submarine zones and mine fields. She arrived in Helsinki, Finland, just as the Russians attacked. "War started at nine o'clock promptly," she wrote. "The people of Helsinki stood in the streets and listened to the painful rising and falling and always louder wail of the sirens. For the first time in history they heard the sound of bombs falling on their city."

In December 1939, Martha Gellhorn left Europe. "I was despairing for Europe," she later wrote. "The powers of evil and money ruled the world."

(Opposite page) Thérèse Bonney, a photographer, conducted "truth raids" to photograph conflicts in Europe: "I go forth alone, try to get the truth and then bring it back and try to make others face and do something about it." In 1939, she covered the Russian invasion of Finland. During several bombing missions, Bonney risked her life to help the wounded and was awarded medals for her bravery. Her "truth raids" were featured in the wartime comic book True Comics, *pictured at left.*

Chapter 3

EUROPE GOES TO WAR

Martha Gellhorn went to Cuba to write a novel and to live with Ernest Hemingway, whom she eventually married. They had been war correspondents in Spain together. In Cuba, they wrote novels based on what they had witnessed in war-torn Europe. He wrote *For Whom the Bell Tolls,* set during the Spanish civil war. She wrote *A Stricken Field,* set in Czechoslovakia. While they were writing in Cuba, Hitler was unleashing his military might in Europe.

Between March and June of 1940, Germany had conquered six countries—Denmark, Norway, Belgium, Luxembourg, the Netherlands, and France.

Virginia Cowles left Paris hours before German troops arrived. She was stranded until a male correspondent agreed to take her in his car. Driving southward out of Paris, they joined hordes of fleeing people. "Try to think in terms of millions," wrote Virginia Cowles. "Try to think of noise and confusion, of the thick smell

Roads clogged with French refugees fleeing the Nazi invasion of Paris in 1940.

of petrol, of the scraping of automobile gears, of shouts, wails, curses. Try to think of a hot sun and underneath it an unbroken stream of humanity....There were some people in carts, some on foot and some on bicycles. But for the most part...anything that had four wheels and an engine was pressed into service...taxicabs, ice-trucks, bakery vans, perfume wagons, sports roadsters and Paris buses....I even saw a hearse loaded with children."

Sonia Tomara also barely escaped from Paris. She traveled by car, rode in a truck, and walked in rain with her sleeping bag and typewriter to get to Tours. There she found a French government censor, whose stamp of approval had to be on a dispatch before the wire operator would cable it.

Tomara's story appeared on the front page of the *New York Herald Tribune*. "For four days and four nights," she wrote, "I have shared the appalling hardship of 5,000,000 French refugees.... As I finish this story there is a German air raid. The sound of bombs is terrific. Like the other refugees, and there are millions of us, I do not know tonight when I shall sleep in a bed again, or how I shall get out of town."

Sonia Tomara in uniform. Her article on the invasion of Paris ran on the front page of the New York Herald Tribune.

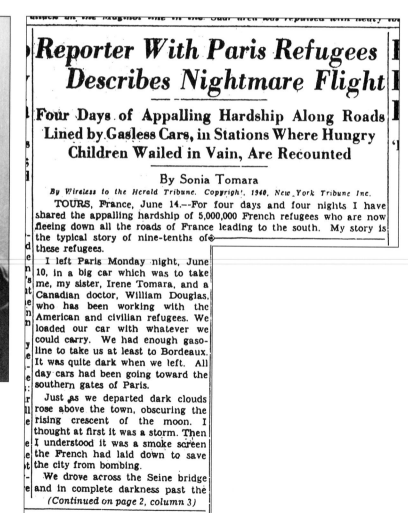

Reporter With Paris Refugees Describes Nightmare Flight

Four Days of Appalling Hardship Along Roads Lined by Gasless Cars, in Stations Where Hungry Children Wailed in Vain, Are Recounted

By Sonia Tomara

By Wireless to the Herald Tribune. Copyright, 1940, New York Tribune Inc.

TOURS, France, June 14.--For four days and four nights I have shared the appalling hardship of 5,000,000 French refugees who are now fleeing down all the roads of France leading to the south. My story is the typical story of nine-tenths of these refugees.

I left Paris Monday night, June 10, in a big car which was to take me, my sister, Irene Tomara, and a Canadian doctor, William Douglas, who has been working with the American and civilian refugees. We loaded our car with whatever we could carry. We had enough gasoline to take us at least to Bordeaux. It was quite dark when we left. All day cars had been going toward the southern gates of Paris.

Just as we departed dark clouds rose above the town, obscuring the rising crescent of the moon. I thought at first it was a storm. Then I understood it was a smoke screen the French had laid down to save the city from bombing.

We drove across the Seine bridge and in complete darkness past the

(Continued on page 2, column 3)

Eventually, Tomara made her way to Portugal and then by ship to New York City. Virginia Cowles got to Le Verdon, a port near Bordeaux. A British cargo boat had been diverted there from its regular route to pick up refugees. Sixteen hundred people, including Cowles and about 60 other correspondents, were crammed onto a ship that normally carried 180 passengers.

"It was difficult to decide where to sleep," Cowles wrote, "for although it was preferable below in case of bombs, it was wiser above in case of torpedoes." She and three male colleagues flipped a coin. The top deck won. They had just put down their blankets when a German plane dropped some bombs, which fortunately missed.

Three days later, the ship arrived in England. Cowles found a country braced for an air attack and determined to win. In a radio broadcast over the British Broadcasting Corporation (BBC) to the United States, she said, "Reports current in America that England will be forced to negotiate a compromise—which means surrender—are unfounded and untrue."

In July 1940, German planes started bombing British airfields and seaports. The Battle of Britain had begun. Although greatly outnumbered, Britain's Royal Air Force fought back heroically.

At first, most of the air battles took place high above the Atlantic Ocean. Helen Kirkpatrick, a correspondent for the *Chicago Daily News*, was among the many people who went to Dover to watch. She had already published two books and a highly respected newsletter about world events when the publisher of the *Chicago Daily News* told her that he wanted to hire her. But, he had said, "we don't have women on the staff." To which Kirkpatrick had replied, "I can't change my sex, but you can change your policy." He did not change his policy, but for her, he made an exception.

Virginia Cowles broadcasting over the BBC from London.

After one of her trips to Dover, Kirkpatrick reported, "Walking about on the cliff above the shore with its rows of neat gardens below, under the warm summer sun and the bright blue sea beyond, with the butterflies fluttering about and the gulls making heathenish noises, it is impossible to feel that there is actually bitter war going on overhead."

That feeling changed abruptly the day a German plane went astray and dropped bombs on London. A church was destroyed and several people were killed. In retaliation, Prime Minister Winston Churchill ordered British pilots to bomb Berlin. Hitler countered with nightly bombing raids on London that became known as the Blitz.

For fifty-six nights, hundreds of German planes dropped bombs on London. Night after night, sirens sounded and giant searchlights swept the sky, illuminating German planes for British antiaircraft gunners. Day after day, rescue parties hauled wounded people and dead bodies out of the smoldering rubble of houses and buildings. In search of safety, people slept in cellars and subway stations.

After spending the second night of the Blitz in a friend's cellar, Helen Kirkpatrick reported, "London still stood this morning, which was the greatest surprise to me, as I cycled home in the light of early dawn after the most frightening night I have ever spent." In covering the Blitz, Kirkpatrick rode in ambulances and fire trucks. "The fires were huge, monstrous," she reported. She regularly sent as many as five cablegrams a day to the *Daily News* in Chicago.

During the Blitz, millions of Americans listened to Edward R. Murrow's nightly broadcasts from London. In the background, listeners could often hear the wail of fire trucks, air raid sirens, and bombs exploding. Murrow, head of the Columbia Broadcasting System (CBS) in London, had wanted to hire Helen Kirkpatrick. Her voice, he explained, was "low-pitched and decisive; more important, she was one of the best correspondents in London." But Murrow had already hired Mary Marvin Breckinridge, so his bosses said no to Kirkpatrick. One woman was enough.

Breckinridge, who used Marvin as her first name, was the first woman foreign broadcaster for a radio network. Using the new shortwave transmitter, which could carry broadcasts farther, Breckinridge reported from various cities, including Berlin, before the United States entered the war. "Your stuff so far has been first-rate," Murrow once told her. "I am pleased, New York is pleased, and so far as I know, the listeners are pleased. If they aren't, to hell with them."

Martha Gellhorn followed the war from Cuba. She wrote, "Far off, safe in the sun, I listened to the radio, a daily funeral bell." Gellhorn put up wall maps and marked Hitler's advances and conquests.

During the summer of 1940, Italy entered the war on

Mary Marvin Breckinridge at work in Holland in 1940. Below, her press credentials for covering the action in France and Germany.

Germany's side; that winter, it attacked Greece. Betty Wason covered the fighting for *Newsweek* and CBS radio. Wason, who grew up in a small town in Indiana, had already broadcast from Czechoslovakia, Hungary, Rumania, and Norway. She sneaked past border guards to get into Norway and hid in the woods to escape bombs and machine-gun fire.

When Greek soldiers pushed the Italians back deep into Albania, Wason followed them. There she slept in ambulances, in trucks, and on the floor in her sleeping bag alongside soldiers and male war correspondents.

When the Italians were unable to defeat the Greeks, the Germans joined in. During the German assault of Athens, Wason wrote five scripts a day that had to be approved by six censors. Her final broadcast was the day after the Germans captured Athens and flew the swastika, the symbol of the Nazi Party, from the Parthenon.

Getting out of Athens was not easy. Finally, Wason and two other American correspondents were allowed to fly to Vienna, Austria, on a German plane. In Vienna, German officials suspected them of being spies and took them under Gestapo (the Nazi secret police) guard to Berlin. Although the other correspondents were soon released, Wason was held a week. When she returned to America, CBS told her that they did not use women broadcasters in the United States.

In early 1941, Wason and other women war correspondents were honored by the New York Newspaper Women's Club at its annual Front Page Ball. The ball was dedicated to "the coterie of women under fire, turning out their daily dispatches as competently as the men beside whom they work."

Chapter 4

THE UNITED STATES
GOES TO WAR

Margaret Bourke-White was the only foreign photographer in the Soviet Union when Hitler ordered tanks, planes, and three million soldiers to invade in June 1941. Although there had been warning signs that Hitler would violate his alliance with Stalin, the Soviets were unprepared. The massive German force quickly advanced deep into Russia.

Bourke-White had been there since early May, after flying from Los Angeles to Hong Kong to Moscow. The trip from Hong Kong to Moscow across China, then at war with Japan, took thirty-one days because of sandstorms, mechanical failures, and missed connections. Fortunately, in addition to five cameras, twenty-two lenses, three thousand flashbulbs, and four portable developing tanks, Bourke-White had packed twenty-eight detective stories, which helped her pass the time.

Bourke-White took great risks photographing the German

night bombing of Moscow. When the air raid alarm sounded, everyone in Moscow was under orders to take shelter in the subway stations, but Bourke-White ignored the order.

First she took pictures from the roof of the deserted American embassy. Then she moved to a hotel and set up her cameras on the balcony and windowsill. She developed the film in her bathtub. When wardens came around to make sure everyone had evacuated the hotel during a raid, Bourke-White hid under her bed. Focusing on photography rather than the danger, she marveled at the sight of the tracer bullets and magnesium flares in the sky. "It was as though the German pilots and the Russian antiaircraft gunners had been handed enormous brushes dipped in radium paint and were executing abstract designs with the sky as their canvas," she wrote.

Before she left Russia, Bourke-White finally got to where the ground action was. Although there was a law against women going to the front lines, she got permission to go by convincing Russian officials that she was doing "the work of men."

On the way there, Bourke-White was staying at a hotel where a bomb killed four members of one family. She was at the scene with her camera. "It is a peculiar thing about pictures of this sort," she wrote. "It is as though a protecting screen draws itself across my mind and makes it possible to consider focus and light values and the technique of photography. . . . This blind lasts as long as it is needed—while I am actually operating the camera."

But when the mother of another dead girl arrived, Bourke-White acknowledged that her "desperate moans penetrated even my protective shell, and as I focused my camera on this vision of human misery, it seemed heartless to turn her suffering into a photograph. But war is war and it has to be recorded."

Bourke-White left Russia in September. Three months later, on

Margaret Bourke-White's dramatic photograph of the Kremlin in Moscow lit up by Russian antiaircraft tracer bullets and German magnesium flares used to provide light for their nighttime bombing raid. Bourke-White took this picture from her hotel balcony.

December 7, 1941, Japanese dive-bombers, torpedo planes, and fighters attacked the U.S. naval base at Pearl Harbor in Hawaii. Caught by surprise, the U.S. fleet was devastated—2,403 Americans died, 5 battleships sank, other ships were severely damaged, and 200 planes were destroyed. The next day, the U.S. Congress voted for a formal declaration of war on Japan. Several days later, Germany and Italy joined Japan and declared war on the United States, and the United States declared war on Germany and Italy.

America's entry into the war changed the way American correspondents and photographers did their jobs. Now those who wanted to cover a war zone had to be accredited by the United States War Department's public relations office. First, correspondents had to get their employer—a newspaper, magazine, news association, or radio network—to agree to send them to cover the war and pay their salary. Then the employer submitted a long application for each journalist, and the intelligence section of the army thoroughly investigated each applicant. Once approved, correspondents received an honorary rank of captain, which, if they were captured by the enemy, would ensure them certain protections. Later in the war, correspondents entered with the rank of major.

Accredited war correspondents received inoculations and equipment—uniforms, a helmet, a gas mask, a bedroll, a spade, and two musette bags, or canvas bags with a strap. Uniforms and personal items went in one musette bag. Typewriter, cameras, and other writing or photography supplies went in the other. Their press credentials were inserted in a little green leather- or canvas-backed card, folded over three times.

At first, war correspondents wore a green armband with a

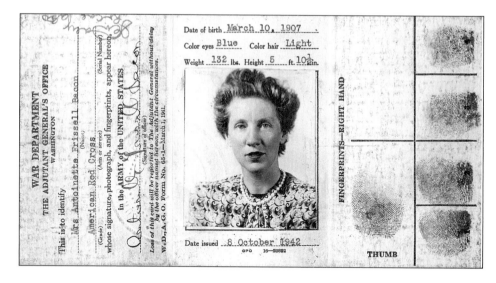

Toni Frissell, a fashion photographer for Vogue *and* Harper's Bazaar, *got her press credentials in 1942. She explained her reasons for wanting to cover the war: "I became so frustrated with fashions that I wanted to prove to myself that I could do a real reporting job."*

large white letter *C* for *correspondent* or *P* for *photographer*. In combat, however, the large white letters became a target, and the armband was replaced with a rectangular patch reading "War Correspondent" over the left jacket pocket and a circular patch on the cap. Later in the war, veteran correspondents wore brass insignias with the phrase "War Correspondent."

Men routinely obtained accreditation; women were typically denied it. The women were told that there were no facilities for them. That they were not physically strong enough. That they would distract the soldiers. That war was a male subject. That the Articles of War established by the U.S. Army forbade women from going into combat.

Given these policies and attitudes, Martha Gellhorn decided to stay in Cuba. In a letter to First Lady Eleanor Roosevelt, she expressed her desire to cover the war and her anger that women were prohibited from covering combat. If she could become a man, she wrote, she would. But since she could not, she would stay at home with Hemingway.

Margaret Bourke-White was the first woman to obtain accreditation to the U.S. Army Air Forces after her employer, *Life*, agreed to let the War Department use her photographs for publicity purposes. In the spring of 1942, she went to England to photograph the arrival of the B-17s, big, heavy bombers known as Flying Fortresses. Determined to photograph an actual bombing mission, she repeatedly asked for permission to fly on a combat mission. Her request was always denied, although several male correspondents went. Even after one male correspondent died in a plane crash, Bourke-White remained determined. The only question in her mind was when the military would let her go.

Sonia Tomara obtained accreditation in August 1942 after Helen Rogers Reid, the powerful publisher of the *New York Herald Tribune*, exerted pressure on the War Department. Assigned to the China-Burma-India (CBI) theater, Tomara covered a disastrous hurricane, revolts in India, and the plight of hordes of refugees fleeing the Japanese in Burma.

Like Bourke-White, Tomara wanted to go on a bombing mission. Knowing that male correspondents were authorized to go, Tomara asked General Joseph W. Stilwell for permission. She made her request during a press conference, and Stilwell, the commander of all U.S. forces in the CBI theater, replied with one word, "Nope!"—at which point the male correspondents laughed.

Tomara was not as bothered by their laughter as she was by being denied an opportunity to do her job just because she was a woman. That made her furious. Her newspaper had not sent her to CBI to be handicapped by her sex. The question was what to do that would not result in the loss of her accreditation.

The war went badly for the Allies during the first six months of 1942. The Japanese gained control of Hong Kong, Singapore,

Malaya, Burma, and Thailand and were advancing toward Australia. The German army was marching toward Stalingrad. German field marshal Erwin Rommel was unchecked in North Africa. German U-boats virtually controlled the North Atlantic.

By midsummer, however, the news got better. The U.S. Navy won two crucial naval battles and slowed the Japanese advance in the Pacific. In the fall, the Russians launched an extraordinary defense of Stalingrad that would eventually defeat the Germans. In November, the Allies launched Operation Torch, the invasion of North Africa.

Margaret Bourke-White had gotten permission to go to North Africa. However, military officials refused to let her fly. It was too dangerous, they said. Instead, in December 1942, she sailed on a troopship carrying nurses that was part of a large convoy.

In the early hours of the morning on December 22, a torpedo hit the ship. "The torpedo did not make as loud a crash as I had expected," Bourke-White wrote, "nor did the ship list as much as it does in the movies. But somehow everyone on the sleeping transport knew almost instantly that this was the end of her."

Bourke-White managed to save two of her six cameras and some film. She hoped to take pictures of the sinking ship, but when she realized that it was too dark, she headed for her lifeboat. As required, the other ships in the convoy sailed away to avoid being torpedoed. Two destroyers stayed behind to drop depth charges on the German submarine, not to rescue people. The hundreds of people packed into seventeen lifeboats would have to wait.

In Bourke-White's crowded lifeboat, people rowed, bailed water with their helmets, and threw up as the boat tossed about. For a time, they heard a voice crying out in the distance, "I am all alone! I am all alone." Unable to steer their lifeboat because the

This photograph by Toni Frissell was used by the American Red Cross on their posters. She covered the war for them as well as the Women's Army Corps and the Eighth Army Air Force, and probably was the only professional photographer to cover the elite African American fighter pilots of the segregated 332nd Fighter Group.

Helen Kirkpatrick interviewing the first American troops in Ireland in 1942. The soldiers wore helmets from World War I because the U.S. had just entered the war and did not yet have new equipment.

rudder had broken, Bourke-White wrote, they listened as "the cry drifted farther and farther away until it was lost in distant silence."

After about eight hours, a destroyer rescued them. Once aboard, Bourke-White photographed "the last of our family of lifeboats as their occupants were helped to the deck." There were two soldiers who had died of injuries, nurses with "sprained ankles, twisted arms and broken legs." Then there was a soldier sitting alone on a raft. Bourke-White reported that "he raised his thumb toward our destroyer and shouted, 'Hi, taxi!'"

New York World-Telegram

7TH SPORTS
FINAL
SEVENTH RACE
THREE CENTS IN CITY
Elsewhere Four Cents

Local Forecast: Tonight rain, not quite as cool as last night. Sunset, 5:30 p. m.; dimout, 6 p. m.

VOL. 75—NO. 129—IN TWO SECTIONS—SECTION ONE   NEW YORK, TUESDAY, DECEMBER 1, 1942.

NONSTOP AIR ASSAULT BLASTS AXIS IN TUNISIA

Chapter 5

ACTION IN NORTH AFRICA AND CHINA

Margaret Bourke-White's clothes had gone down with the ship. When she arrived in Algiers in late December 1942, General James H. (Jimmy) Doolittle, commander of the U.S. Army Air Forces in North Africa, loaned her some of his. He also gave her permission to fly on a bombing mission. After all, he said, she had survived being torpedoed.

Bourke-White spent a week in the desert heat getting ready. Wearing layers of clothing under a bulky fleece-lined leather flying suit, an oxygen mask, and the electric mittens that were required for high-altitude flying, she practiced maneuvering her bulky aerial cameras inside a B-17. To protect her film from the heat, she buried it under six feet of sand.

Bourke-White was in the lead plane when thirty-two B-17s took off to bomb the airfield at Tunis, the main base of the German Luftwaffe in North Africa. Using a portable oxygen bottle, she

On January 27, 1943, Margaret Bourke-White became the first woman to accompany the U.S. Air Force on a bombing mission. This photograph appeared in Life, *and it became a favorite of American soldiers, who pinned it up in their quarters.*

moved around the plane, shooting photos from every window. She followed the bombardier into the cramped bomb bay and photographed him removing the safety pins from the bombs. Her plane was hit twice, but the damage was light. Two B-17s, however, were shot down. During that raid, many German planes were destroyed.

Doolittle's decision to let Bourke-White go on a bombing mission almost got him demoted. But her photos and article in *Life* provided such great publicity that his superiors just grumbled to themselves. It would be a while, however, before Bourke-White would be allowed back in a combat zone. While the military loved the dramatic press coverage, it did not like anyone, especially a woman, who evaded the public relations office regulations or broke rules in other ways.

Meanwhile, in CBI, Sonia Tomara managed to go on a bombing mission, too. Despite Stilwell's abrupt rejection of her request, she later wrote an article praising him. "What are those lies you have written about me?" Stilwell joked when they met at a dinner party. "Come and collect the pay someday."

That day came when she had moved to another section of CBI and got permission to go on a bombing raid from Stilwell's subordinate, General Claire Chennault, U.S. air commander in China.

Tomara flew aboard a B-25, a midsize bomber. "Bombers are not comfortable means of transportation. I sat on my heels behind the pilots and looked at the country through the windshield," she later wrote. She also shared an oxygen mask with the bombardier. Seeing bombs drop out of the planes around her, she deliberately did not look down at the destruction.

While Tomara was congratulated by her boss at the *New York Herald Tribune*, a military public relations officer chewed her out and reported her to Stilwell. Afraid of being disaccredited, Tomara wrote Stilwell a profuse apology. "Let us forget about it, Sonia," he replied in a handwritten note. "We all think that you are a good newspaperman, and we like you."

By 1943, it had become slightly easier for women to get accredited—but only to cover the so-called women's angle, such as the activities of nurses and members of the newly created branches of the military for women. Even then, women correspondents faced opposition.

Sonia Tomara Flies in a Raid Over Hankow

Sees Bomber Unload on Yangtse City Airdrome After Escorts Clear Way

By Sonia Tomara
By Wireless to the Herald Tribune
Copyright, 1943, New York Tribune Inc.

WITH FORWARD ECHELON OF 14TH AIR FORCE, China, Aug. 22 (Delayed.)—American Liberators swept over the Japanese-held base at Hankow, on the Yangtse River north of here, yesterday, fired the docks and dispersal areas and destroyed thirty-five of fifty intercepting Zeros, leaving the foe powerless before succeeding waves of Mitchell bombers, which were able to drop their bombs without fighter opposition.

I happened to be in one of the Mitchells, which did their work accurately and swiftly. We met anti-aircraft fire but no Japanese fighters. I saw our bombs go down in clusters on revetments and hangars of a Japanese pursuit group. We were prepared to fight, but our guns remained silent. It would have been a different story had I been aboard one of the Liberators.

The four-engined B-24's met fierce resistance as they roared over to drop thirty tons of bombs on their Hankow targets. The effectiveness of their blow was confirmed by the Mitchells in their follow-up attack.

One Liberator went down in flames—the first loss suffered in combat by these planes in this theater. Some of the men who bailed out when the ship caught fire were machine-gunned by Japanese fighters and probably were killed. I cannot disclose their names as their families must be informed first.

Sonia Tomara's firsthand account of a bombing raid over Hankow, China, appeared on the front page of the New York Herald Tribune.

Ruth Cowan, of the Associated Press (AP), and Inez Robb, of the International News Service (INS), were accredited and attached to the first two companies of the Women's Army Auxiliary Corps to be sent overseas. When they arrived in Casablanca, French Morocco, Wes Gallagher, head of the Algiers bureau of the AP, was furious. "Put them on the boat and send them back," he said, and after that, he gave Cowan the silent treatment.

When she went to the press corps dining room, the Frenchman who ran it refused to serve her. That did not bother Cowan, she

Ruth Cowan covered the war for the Associated Press. The C on her armband stood for "correspondent."

later said. "My meals were served in my room, and I ate a helluva lot better than the men did." Although the chief of INS treated Robb better, General Robert McClure, a U.S. Army public relations officer in Algiers, was hostile to both women.

Cowan had broken into journalism in the 1920s by writing under the byline R. Baldwin Cowan. Based in Austin, Texas, she was working for the United Press (UP). She got fired the day a UP executive called to praise Cowan for *his* work and discovered that he was a she. UP, Cowan was told, did not hire women. When she wired an AP executive with the news that she had been fired because she was a woman, he immediately hired her.

An AP Washington correspondent as of 1940, Cowan was good friends with First Lady Eleanor Roosevelt. With Gallagher and McClure making it impossible for her to do her job, she sent a cable to Eleanor Roosevelt that read: "Don't encourage more women to come to Africa. The men don't want us here."

Cowan knew that the military censors would undoubtedly stop the transmission of her cable. However, she figured that even the remote possibility of such a message getting to the powerful and outspoken First Lady might bring about a change of climate. Her strategy worked, because soon she was invited to attend General Dwight D. Eisenhower's press conference. Eisenhower was then commander of the Allied forces in North Africa. He was acutely aware of the importance of good public relations in fighting a war. It was the key, he said, to keeping up civilian and military morale and support for the war.

In February, Cowan and Robb got permission to fly to the front lines. The military did not expect the plane to encounter any combat. However, it landed in the middle of the American army in retreat after a surprise attack by German forces. In the chaos, the plane took off without Cowan, Robb, and the officers who had accompanied them. The officers stood helpless, watching trucks loaded with soldiers speeding by. Cowan and Robb, however, stuck out their thumbs and hitched a ride from a truck driver from Montana.

Cowan arrived back in Algiers just in time to attend a reception at the French embassy. "I was tired. I smelled. I was dirty," she recalled. "Once in uniform, you stayed in uniform, and if you

stank, you stank." General George S. Patton, commander of the Third Army, was at the reception, too. An aggressive, flamboyant man, Patton confronted Cowan: "So," he asked her, "you want to be in the war? What is the first law of war?"

Without hesitation, she replied, "You kill him before he kills you."

"She stays," he announced.

Throughout her career, Cowan knew that being told she could "write like a man" was the highest praise. Now AP editors in New York were using her war writing as an example of the best. "Why can't you write the way she does?" the editors wrote in a cable that was sent to male AP correspondents in North Africa.

(Opposite page) Clare Boothe Luce, a war correspondent for Life, *interviewed General "Vinegar Joe" Stilwell (far left) in 1942 at his headquarters in Burma. She described war-torn Europe as "a world where men have decided to die together because they are unable to find a way to live together." The painted headlights on the Chevrolet were for wartime black-outs, when any light visible at night might draw bombers.*

Chapter 6

GETTING TO ITALY

Martha Gellhorn returned to the war in the fall of 1943. Since Pearl Harbor, she had tried to get Hemingway to leave Cuba with her and cover the war. He was too busy, he said, using his fishing boat to search for U-boats in the waters off Cuba.

Finally, it became impossible for Gellhorn "to sit on the outside and watch." She contacted *Collier's* and set about getting accredited. "War is a malignant disease," she once wrote, "an idiocy, a prison, and the pain it causes is beyond our telling or imagining; but war was our condition and our history, the place we had to live."

Gellhorn arrived in London in November. One of the first things she did was have breakfast with Virginia Cowles, her old friend from the days when they both had covered the Spanish civil war. Now Cowles was assistant to the American ambassador in London. In a flurry of activity, Gellhorn wrote articles about

English pilots and Dutch refugees and accounts of atrocities against Jews, her visits to burn wards in hospitals, and her conversations with children. "They have never bought food except with ration books, or clothes without coupons," she wrote of the children who had known only war throughout their lives. "They

Margaret Bourke-White at an observation point in Italy. Three of her cameras are set up to photograph action in the Cassino valley.

grew up to find trenches in playgrounds, bunks in the subway, queues for everything, and they have never had a date except in the blackout."

Shortly before Gellhorn arrived in London, Italy had surrendered to the Allies and declared war on Germany. Heavily armed German troops, however, were entrenched in Italy, and dislodging them was turning out to be difficult. In November, the difficulty was compounded by constant rain, which turned the ground into knee-deep mud. Sometimes it seemed as if the American Fifth Army and British Eighth Army were moving through the valleys and mountain gaps inch by inch, if at all.

Helen Kirkpatrick was in Italy with an American mobile surgical unit. When she was not writing articles, she was helping out. "Amputations didn't bother me—I could tolerate anything as long as I didn't see the face of the man," she wrote.

Despite great difficulty in getting permission from the military, Margaret Bourke-White had arrived in Italy in October. There she met Major Maxwell Jerome Papurt, the officer in charge of giving her a pass to get to the front lines. Papurt, a fan of her work, readily gave her the pass. She traveled by jeep to the front lines and shot photos as shells fell around her. She flew reconnaissance missions low over enemy territory in an unarmed, slow two-seater plane dubbed a Grasshopper. Once, German fighters attacked the plane. Yelling at her to hang on and tighten her seat belt, the pilot took evasive action, which he later described as "rapid changes in altitude and direction—rather violent corkscrew dives." Quickly looking over his shoulder to reassure Bourke-White, he was astonished to see her calmly taking photos of the German planes.

After the war, the pilot remembered of Bourke-White, "I was most impressed by Peggy's coolness and asked her [after they

Doris Fleeson, war correspondent for Woman's Home Companion, *talking with two American soldiers in their foxhole on the Italian front.*

landed], 'Peggy, you are either the bravest person I've ever known or a damn fool—which are you?' She gave me that intense blue-eyed look and that mischievous grin and said, 'Which do you think I am?'"

Martha Gellhorn went to Italy in February of 1944. By hooking up with French forces, she got around the frontline restrictions of her U.S. accreditation. "I had been sent to Europe to do my job, which was not to report the rear areas or the woman's angle," she later wrote.

Riding in a jeep with a French soldier, she traveled through snow and hail on narrow, slippery roads up mountains where the Germans were well entrenched. "From time to time," she wrote, "we would pass a completely unnecessary sign: a skull-and-bones painted on a board, with underneath the phrase in French, 'The enemy sees you.' No one needed to be warned. There you were, on a roller-coaster of a road freezing to death, and if the enemy couldn't see you, he was blind; he was sitting right across there, on that other snowy mountain."

The army air force sent Toni Frissell on a tour of combat areas in Europe to take pictures that would get the story "not only told, but understood." Ankle-deep in mud and holding her camera, she is standing with two officers in front of a tank.

Gellhorn described an endless stream of "trucks and jeeps, command cars and ambulances, wrecking cars and tanks and tank destroyers and munitions carriers." She noted that along the road there was always a soldier shaving: "Naked to the waist in the cold, he wages the losing battle to keep clean." Then there were old women washing clothes in a stone trough, and children swinging on an old telephone wire "hung from a tree in an ammunition dump." She reported her conversation with a doctor at a first-aid station about minefields: "'Think about it,' he said, 'for

The daring exploits of Martha Gellhorn, who is referred to as Mrs. Ernest Hemingway, were the subject of this front-page article in the St. Louis Post-Dispatch.

Martha Gellhorn Sets Out to See Cassino; Shot At, Dives Into Ditch

Venture Goes Well Till Her Party Comes Under Guns and Is Turned Back — Germans' Aim Is Bad.

By WILLIAM H. STONEMAN
The Chicago Daily News—Post-Dispatch Special Radio. Copyright, 1944.

NEAR CASSINO, Feb. 14 (delayed). — Mrs. Ernest Hemingway (the former Martha Gellhorn, daughter of Mrs. George Gellhorn of St. Louis) had decided that she wanted to cross the river into the outskirts of Cassino. She had been there before, some time ago, and was deeply suspicious of warnings that crossing had become too hot for tourist traffic. In a weak moment we volunteered to go along with her and check up on the situation.

To reach this crossing you drive along a road paralleling the Rapido River bed until you are practically in Cassino, then turn sharp right and dash across a short stretch of road into a shelter of cliffs on the other side. For the last half mile or so you are under

MARTHA GELLHORN HEMINGWAY

direct observation by the Germans, practically under the nose of Larocca, the enemy-held castle just above Cassino itself. The crossroads where you turn off to cross the river has long been conceded to be a hot spot.

When we reached this spot the

Continued on Page 6, Column 3.

MARTHA GELLHORN STARTS TO CASSINO BUT NAZIS STOP HER
Continued From Page One.

Germans let loose. Mrs. Hemingway hit a nice deep ditch at the same second that we did. There our tour stopped. After a pause of 15 minutes to let the Germans get over their shooting spree, we went into reverse. One lady correspondent and one male rounded the crossroads at a run and did not stop running until it was far behind.

We enjoyed the next few minutes watching various jeeps and quarter-ton trucks running the gantlet. Every time our car came to a turn a few shells would drop neatly beside it. For some fantastic reason nobody seemed to get hit.

Down the road we found our driver, Nobby Clark, eating lunch and making himself at home with five permanent inhabitants of a shattered farmhouse. While we were drinking tea and brandy and catching our breath, we heard a cry from the distance and saw a figure staggering across the nearby field. Two soldiers were out like a flash and came in a few minutes later with an Indian military policeman. He cut off his pants leg and applied enough sulfanilamide powdr and emergency bandages to supply a regiment. All he had wrong with him was about a dozen shell fragments in the leg.

Mrs. Hemingway, a veteran of several previous wars, was not abashed. She was just wondering out loud why we did not go into Cassino. Let her go on wondering.

years after this war, people will be killed all over Europe in such fields; men will be killed sowing their wheat and children will be killed playing. It is horrible. Everything about war is too horrible to consider.'"

That night Gellhorn lay on her cot in the aid station and "listened to the mice and the shells." And she remembered "the dead girl ambulance driver, lying on a bed...with her hands crossed on a sad bunch of flowers....She had been killed on the road below San Elia, and her friends, the other French girls who drove ambulances, were coming to pay their last respects. They were tired and awkward in their bulky, muddy clothes. They passed slowly before the dead girl and looked with pity and great quietness at her face, and went back to their ambulances."

Chapter 7

D-DAY

By 1944, it was clear that an invasion of Europe across the English Channel was imminent. Exactly when and where was top-secret, but a massive buildup of war matériel had been going on in Britain for some time. "Every tree and hedge played its part in a great camouflage. Woods and hedgerows were spiky with guns and jammed tight with vehicles. Towns and villages bristled with men and armor and equipment," was how Iris Carpenter, of the *Boston Globe,* described the scene.

Carpenter was an Englishwoman with an indomitable look in her eyes. Born into great wealth, she was determined to make a name for herself. At the age of eighteen, she entered journalism as a movie critic. Early in the war, a German bomb had landed on her estate. Then five German planes crashed on her property. She got a job with an American newspaper in order to get U.S. accreditation. British field marshal Bernard Montgomery was adamantly opposed to women correspondents. "I will not tolerate them," he said.

"Americans, on the other hand," Carpenter explained, "admitted that 'certain phases of war should be covered by women.'"

Anticipating the invasion, a steady stream of correspondents arrived in London, including more women than ever before. Editors of newspapers, magazines, and news services had begun to hire more women for several reasons. One reason, of course, was that with so many male journalists serving in the military, editors had no choice but to hire women.

But more than that, as John C. Oestreicher, foreign director of the International News Service, pointed out, "prejudice against women as foreign correspondents...disappeared...when from the battlefronts of Europe there suddenly appeared an avalanche

A group of women war correspondents in London. (Left to right) Mary Welsh, Dixie Tighe, Kathleen Harriman, Helen Kirkpatrick, Lee Miller, and Tania Long.

of magnificent copy bearing feminine bylines. . . . To the surprise of virtually everyone in the craft at home, ladies of the press checked in day in and day out with stories that the men correspondents didn't get."

Oestreicher himself hired Lee Carson to go to London. Her good looks and perky personality attracted attention wherever she went. She was labeled "every soldier's pinup girl." Carson played along with that image, but she never let it distract her from doing her job.

In an article in *Look,* Carson explained that "the best break I got in way of preparation for the battlefront came . . . when I was born into a family of outspoken, uninhibited sons." Those sons—her rough-and-tumble brothers—showed her a side of life that many girls never saw.

Lee Carson typing a dispatch in London.

According to Carson, war in the winter meant "inescapable, unrelieved cold; few baths, scabies; trenchfoot; endless rides in topless, windshieldless jeeps that give you a complexion mottled with frostbite; two sets of long underwear; all the sweaters you own, outsize combat pants, four pairs of sox, galoshes...and still you freeze."

On the front lines, she wrote, life "narrows down to an existence divided between fighting to keep alive and sweating out being killed. The longer in the combat world the more improbable that other world—of sweethearts, mothers, baths, beds—becomes. Death, dirt and fatigue are the familiar. All else fades into a dream. Even such strong emotions as fear and hate are eventually wiped out by battle."

Women correspondents, especially those who had covered the Battle of Britain and the fighting in Italy, assumed that they would get permission to cover the invasion. Helen Kirkpatrick was part of the team that spent months planning the logistics for press coverage. In the end, however, the Supreme Headquarters of the Allied Expeditionary Forces (SHAEF) decreed that women war correspondents would not be permitted to cover the invasion of German-occupied France, which would become known as D-Day.

Ignoring the order, Lee Carson managed to get a seat on a fighter plane and got an aerial view of the invasion of the Normandy coast on June 6, 1944. Her dispatch was an exclusive eyewitness report of the invasion, and perhaps the first. SHAEF responded to her daring feat by issuing an order of discipline against her. But she evaded the military police who were assigned to enforce it. Later, Carson was quoted as saying, "Sure, I knew it [the policy that women could not cover combat]. But my job was to get the news."

Martha Gellhorn stowed away on a hospital ship that went to Normandy on June 7, or D-Day plus one. That night, she went ashore with the stretcher bearers to retrieve wounded men. "Everyone was violently busy on that crowded dangerous shore," she wrote. "The pebbles were the size of melons and we stumbled up a road that a huge road shovel was scooping out. We walked with the utmost care between the narrowly placed white tape lines that marked the mine-cleared path, and headed for a tent marked with a red cross just behind the beach."

The Normandy coast of France on D-Day plus one. Three million Allied soldiers participated in all phases of the invasion.

Gellhorn worked throughout the night helping the stretcher bearers and nurses. They did not even pause during an air raid. Although they could not hear the German planes or any bombs falling, they could hear the *ack-ack* of flak going up at the end of the beach and see it burst in the sky. Gellhorn noted that "the tracers were as lovely as they always are—and no one took pleasure from the beauty of the scene.... Everyone knows flak is a bad thing to have fall on your head."

Shortly after her return to England, Gellhorn was arrested for not having the proper credentials to go into a war zone. She was

Lee Miller, a correspondent for Vogue, *took pictures in a Normandy field hospital shortly after D-Day. (Right) A doctor and nurses performing surgery on a wounded soldier. (Opposite page) Miller's photograph of a soldier being loaded into an evacuation plane headed for England on an airstrip behind the Omaha beachhead in Normandy.*

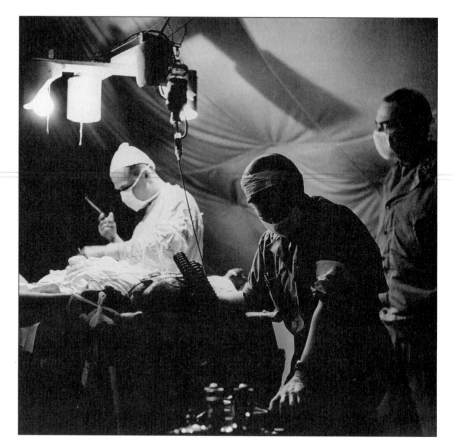

confined to a nurses' training camp. That lasted a day before she scaled a wire fence, hitched a ride to a military airfield, and got on a flight to Italy by convincing the pilot that she was going to meet her fiancé. She left with "no papers, no travel orders, no PX rights, nothing." Gellhorn later said, "I was a gypsy in that war in order to report it."

Iris Carpenter got to Normandy on D-Day plus four. She flew over in the first ambulance plane to land on an airstrip that the Allies had finally captured. Carpenter was allowed to go because some military officials wanted to make up to her for having

misled her into believing that she would be allowed to cover the invasion. On the return flight, she interviewed wounded soldiers. That night she broadcast the soldiers' views of the invasion on the BBC nine o'clock news.

A few days later she returned by ship with orders to visit a beachhead. Interpreting the beachhead to include the nearby city of Cherbourg, Carpenter hitched a ride there. In Cherbourg, she visited hospitals, where she found that "the stench of death still hung so heavily you could almost reach a hand out and touch it." In one hospital, Carpenter reported, "a freckle-faced nurse, named Irene York from Nebraska, stripped the garden of lilies and orange blossoms to mass great crocks of them in the wards so the men could bear to breathe."

For her trip, Carpenter was court-martialed, and the outcome depended on the definition of the beachhead. One judge, the chief of British public relations—a "vicious, pompous" officer,

Carpenter later recalled—defined it as a "few square yards of sand." However, the American colonel in charge of the beachhead said that it included Cherbourg, and the case against Carpenter was dismissed—at which point, Carpenter noted, "veins bulged" in the British officer's forehead, and he announced, "'My dear woman, it will be a long while before you get more orders for Normandy—a VERY long while.'"

"But I've got them," she replied, having already obtained them from the American colonel.

(Opposite page) Women war correspondents went with the first contingent of WACs (Women's Army Corps) that crossed the English Channel. Their camp was set up in an apple orchard near Valogne. The women slept on canvas cots and shared an eight-hole latrine. In nice weather, the correspondents wrote their stories on a table under the trees. (Left to right) Virginia Irwin of the St. Louis Post-Dispatch, *Marjorie "Dot" Avery of the* Detroit Free Press, *and Judy Barden, a British reporter.*

Fair, Cool
BOSTON AND VICINITY—Fair
and cool today and tonight. High
4:59 A. M. 5:21 P. M. Low
11:09 A. M. 11:42 P. M.
Sunrise, 6:03. Sunset, 7:57. Full report Page 2.

VOL. CLXXXXVII, NO. 57

THE BOSTON HERALD LATE CITY EDITION

[Copyright, 1944]
Boston Herald-Traveler Corporation

BOSTON, SATURDAY, AUGUST 26, 1944—TWELVE PAGES ★★★★★ THREE CENTS

ALLIES SWEEP TO 3 VICTORIES
Take Troyes, Paris, Push Foe into Seine

Chapter 8

ACTION IN EUROPE

As the U.S. Army moved across northern France, SHAEF issued new orders regarding women war correspondents. Now they had to get the approval of a military public relations officer (PRO) before they could write about anything except nurses or the Women's Army Corps. They could not advance any farther forward than the nurses. They had to stay with the nurses instead of in the press camp. That meant they were denied access to what the male correspondents had: twice-daily press briefings, military maps, jeeps and drivers, an on-the-spot censor, and facilities for teletype and radio transmission.

While some women accepted these rules, other women continued to find ways to get to where the action was.

Lee Miller, of *Vogue*, did it accidentally.

The Eighty-third Division of the U.S. Army had captured the seaside town of St. Malo, France. At least that was what the PRO believed, and he sent Miller there to photograph the Civil Affairs team, which helped civilians adjust after the fighting. Traveling alone, Miller hitched a ride to St. Malo and discovered that the Germans had not surrendered.

Although she was not accredited to be in combat, she was not about to leave. "I had the clothes I was standing in, a couple dozen films, and an eiderdown blanket roll," Miller wrote. "I was the only photographer for miles around and I now owned a private war." Fortunately, the Civil Affairs team and the American soldiers were unfazed by her presence.

Lee Miller camped with the nurses of the Forty-fourth Evac Hospital in Normandy. She photographed them washing up.

She photographed soldiers directing mortar fire, soldiers getting ready to go into action with "grenades hanging on their lapels like Cartier clips," and soldiers dying. She captured bomb bursts on film as well as a soldier sharing his chocolate rations with a group of children. Finally, she photographed the Germans' surrender at St. Malo.

Without realizing it, Miller also photographed one of the first times napalm, a top-secret weapon, was used in an air attack. When the censor in London saw those photos, he immediately seized them.

The editors at *Vogue* were thrilled with Miller's photos and text. Her story was featured in the October issue of both the American and the British editions of *Vogue,* along with stories on the latest fashions. The PRO, however, had her placed under house arrest for violating the terms of her accreditation.

The first day of her confinement, Miller slept. The next three days, she typed nonstop. Then she slipped away and headed for Paris. Allied forces were pushing the Germans out of France. Paris was about to be liberated, and Miller was going to be there when it happened. "I won't be the first woman journalist—in Paris—by any means," she wrote to her editor at *Vogue,* "but I'll be the first dame photographer, I think, unless someone parachutes in."

By the time she was twenty years old, Miller was a top fashion model who regularly appeared on the cover and pages of *Vogue*. In 1929, she moved to Paris and became the protégée and lover of Man Ray, a famous artist and photographer. Together they invented the process of solarization, a darkroom technique that uses light to highlight aspects of a picture. Eventually, Miller moved to London and got a job as a photographer for the British edition of *Vogue*.

Lee Miller's photograph of a napalm explosion at St. Malo.

(Left) Lee Miller photographed this Normandy village ruined by the fighting. (Right) Miller viewing the devastation with American soldiers on the front at St. Malo.

Miller arrived in Paris the day it was liberated, August 25, 1944. "Paris had gone mad," she wrote. Setting off to find her old friends, she went to the studio of Pablo Picasso, who had spent the war in Paris. "'This is the first Allied soldier I have seen,'" he exclaimed as they fell into each other's arms, "'and it's you!'"

Sonia Tomara was the first woman journalist to arrive in Paris. She rode in a weapons carrier just before the city was liberated. Four years earlier, Tomara had fled Paris, but her sister and close friends had remained. "My heart was so tense," she wrote. "It took me a second to run up the three flights of stairs, and here were my folks, just a little older, a little thinner than when I had left them."

Lee Carson arrived in Paris by jeep with the Fourth Infantry Division. An order to apprehend her had been issued because two weeks earlier she had ditched her PRO escort and gone to where the action was. Although she could not file stories, which would reveal her whereabouts to the PRO, she later reported that during her two weeks in the action, "local resistance forces turned over six German soldiers to me as sole representative of the U.S. Army available at the moment. Amid sneering, swarming mobs, I nervously herded the Germans back through town . . . to American GI's on the opposite side of town."

On her way to the Hotel Scribe, the press camp in Paris, Carson narrowly missed being killed by a German sniper. When she arrived in the lobby, she bumped into a PRO who knew about the order against her. He, however, decided to ignore it and simply said he was glad to see her alive.

Martha Gellhorn came from Italy to Paris. Shortly after the liberation, she was given a tour of tunnels under Paris that the Germans had turned into prisons and torture chambers. "Men and women were shut in here, without blankets or light, and here they lived as long as their bodies could endure," she reported. In agonizing detail, Gellhorn described the methods of torture. "It is necessary to know all this," she wrote, "and to try to imagine these places, because these are the wounds of Paris."

Throughout the fall of 1944, Allied forces scored one victory after another. Clearly, they were going to win the war. But the fighting was far from over.

In Italy, the fighting continued to be fierce, and Nisei GIs, American-born soldiers of Japanese descent, were in the thick of the action.

Early in the war, by order of President Franklin D. Roosevelt, 110,000 Japanese Americans from the West Coast were forced to leave their homes and confined in camps. Many of the Nisei GIs had relatives in those camps; some had themselves been interned in camps until they were allowed to enlist and serve in segregated army units. They encountered racial prejudice throughout their basic training at Camp Shelby, in Mississippi.

The extraordinary heroism of the Nisei combat troops was the

Lyn Crost interviewing Japanese American soldiers in Italy.

During World War II, African Americans faced discrimination in many aspects of American society, including the military. Black soldiers were segregated into labor and service units, often barred from combat, and denied promotions as officers. African Americans challenged discrimination during the war and fought to overcome barriers to racial equality. These photographs capture some of the achievements of African Americans during the war. (Top right) Elizabeth Phillips was the only woman of color to become an accredited war correspondent. In her column in the **Baltimore Afro-American,** she informed readers that racism had prepared her for combat. In the fall of 1944, Phillips traveled to England to cover the war, but soon fell ill and had to return to the United States before she had a chance to report from a combat zone. (Bottom right) Toni Frissell covered the action in Italy of some of the hundreds of black soldiers who served as fighter pilots during the war. Here she has just returned from a flight with Major Roberts on her left. (Bottom left) This image represented the Double Victory campaign, organized to build support for military victory overseas and a victory over discrimination in the United States.

stuff of legend. In the fight at Monte Cassino, they were dubbed the "Purple Heart Battalion" because so many were wounded or killed in action. By the end of the war, the 442nd "Go for Broke" Regimental Combat Team was the most decorated unit of its size and length of service in U.S. history.

Many of the Nisei soldiers were from Hawaii, and late in 1944, the *Honolulu Star-Bulletin* hired Lyn Crost to cover them.

Crost had graduated from Brown University with many honors. When she was offered newspaper jobs only in the women's section, she decided to move to Hawaii, where she finally found a job at the *Honolulu Advertiser*. Later, as an AP correspondent in Washington, Crost met Joseph Farrington, the publisher of the *Honolulu Star-Bulletin*. She informed him of the high casualty rates of the Nisei soldiers. In response, he hired her to cover the war, although his paper had a policy against hiring women.

Crost made sure to include many soldiers' names and hometowns in her dispatches. Like other women correspondents, she knew that oftentimes the only news families got from the front lines about their soldier relatives and friends was through the newspapers. "Her name became a household word," recalled Ted Tsukiyama, who served in the CBI and met Crost after the war. "She made sure she dropped as many names as she could; it had a lot of local interest."

Chapter 9

ADVANCING TOWARD GERMANY

By September 1944, Allied forces were spread across northern Europe. Martha Gellhorn, using "stealth and chicanery," had avoided the PROs and reattached herself to an American unit, the Eighty-second Airborne, led by General James Gavin. He was a savvy leader who parachuted out of airplanes and fought alongside his men. Gavin impressed Gellhorn; she, he later said, impressed him. Wanting his men's feats to get press coverage, and unafraid to have a woman be the one who did it, Gavin welcomed Martha Gellhorn.

Gellhorn was with the Eighty-second when it daringly captured a heavily defended bridge at the town of Nijmegen in the Netherlands. She wrote about how the Dutch in Nijmegen tried to help the Jews. And she reported about the fate of twelve hundred Jews who had been held in a nearby German concentration camp.

One day, the Jews—men, women, and children—were told

they could have showers. "As they had lived in misery and filth for months," Gellhorn reported, "they were very happy. They were ordered to undress and leave their clothes outside, notably they were to leave their shoes. From vents, which looked like air vents, the Germans pumped what they call 'blue gas' into the clean white-tiled bathroom. It appears that this gas works faster on slightly humid naked bodies. In some few minutes, twelve hundred people were dead, but not before the SS guard had heard them scream and had watched them die in what agony we cannot know. Then the shoes were laid out, carefully sorted, and sent back to Germany for use, and before the mass cremations all gold fillings and gold teeth were removed from the corpses.

"We know now of many places where Jews have been gassed to death," Gellhorn's dispatch continued, "we have written of it for a long time. People in Europe could not believe this evil and now they do; and to have lived close to such evil and to have seen, heard, and understood it does something to people which will never be wiped out."

On December 16, 1944, the Allies' advance toward Germany was thrown into turmoil when the Germans launched a surprise attack in the Ardennes Forest in Belgium. Breaking through a weak spot between the American First and Third Armies, the Germans pushed out a bulge in the American line; thus the attack became known as the Battle of the Bulge.

Iris Carpenter and Lee Carson were with the First Army. "The Germans are roaring up nearby roads in their Tiger tanks, zooming down from the pink-streaked winter skies to shower our frontline positions with streams of hot lead, and tearing the world apart with their heavy artillery barrages," Carson reported.

The Battle of the Bulge was fought in horrendous winter

Helen Kirkpatrick in uniform. (Bottom) Because of Kirkpatrick's popularity as a war correspondent, the Chicago Daily News used her image on an advertisement that was displayed on city buses.

A group of correspondents in northern France in 1945. (Left to right) Ruth Cowan, Sonia Tomara, Rosette Hargrove, Betty Knox, Iris Carpenter, and Erika Mann.

weather, the worst in years—blizzards, temperatures below freezing, snowdrifts eight to ten feet deep. The roads were often a sheet of ice. "Smash ups became so routine," Carpenter later wrote, "that it needed Lee Carson to smash up three jeeps in a single week to cause comment and then it was a mere 'better take care, Lee, we're getting short of jeeps.'"

Jack Frankish, of UP, decided to spend Christmas Day in the press camp. The front was too dangerous, he told Carson, Carpenter, and Bill Boni of AP. "I've got a wife and a couple of kids," he said. "I guess I owe something to them as well as my paper."

"Okay," Carson told him. "That's right, if it's the way you feel. I guess that I'll go out, though. I figure if you got it comin', you get it."

Carson, Carpenter, and Boni jeeped to the front. That night they returned to discover that German planes had dive-bombed the press camp. In the attack, Jack Frankish was killed.

By December 27, the Americans had stopped the Germans at Bastogne, a town in Belgium. But on New Year's Day, Carpenter reported, the Luftwaffe launched its most concentrated attack of the war.

Hundreds of German planes attacked and "screamed over the treetops strafing." Despite the freezing cold, soldiers and correspondents alike "shrank into the ground," Carpenter reported. As

Lee Carson's front-page scoop for the New York Journal-American.

GI-Clad Nazis Led Drive in Jeeps

By LEE CARSON,
International News Service Staff Correspondent.

WITH U. S. 1ST ARMY IN BELGIUM, Dec. 20.— Paced by Nazi fanatics who penetrated Belgian towns dressed in United States Army uniforms and driving captured American jeeps. German armored columns assaulting American 1st Army positions today were backed up by infantry troops.

Lt. Gen. Hodges' Army is "strengthening its shoulders" at the northern and southern ends of a 20-mile long German break-through but it has not yet thrown a solid block across the gap.

German columns sped along the roads and infantry troops infiltrated key towns during the night.

LEE CARSON
With Yanks in Belgium

A number of enemy prisoners and dead were found to be wearing civilian clothes.

[The dispatch did not specify whether these men were of the espionage-fighter type parachuted into Holland at the outbreak of the western campaign in 1940, or were members of the Volkssturm, the recently-created Peoples' Army whose forces wear only a distinguishing arm band.]

At one point, the Germans hove into view in possession of four American Sherman tanks which they had captured. One of the crew yelled to Americans nearby "come here" and then opened fire.

On the north "shoulder" of the 1st Army line, counterattacks were beaten off at dawn when American infantry came into contact with the enemy.

Every passing day of this startling German attack brings out disagreeable traits of the enemy.

First Army headquarters announced officially that the Germans are massacring captured Americans. Two instances of the ruthless and cold-blooded murder of disarmed soldiers, predominantly supply troops and medics, were cited.

One occurred near St. Vith, where German troops mounted with .88's ambushed and caught a supply and medical convoy.

The men were disarmed, looted of their personal belongings, included cigarets, and marched into a field. The tank swung its .88 on the men standing with their hands

Continued on Page 2, Column 4.

she lay in the snow, Carpenter's perspiration melted it "to steaming point." William Farr, of the *London Daily Mail,* told her that she generated so much steam, it "put up a smoke screen."

Martha Gellhorn arrived at Bastogne with the Eighty-second Airborne just before New Year's Day. "There were many dead and many wounded," she reported, "but the survivors contained the fluid situation and slowly turned it into a retreat, and finally, as the communiqué said, the bulge was ironed out. This was not done fast or easily; and it was not done by those anonymous things, armies, divisions, regiments. It was done by men, one by one—your men."

Early in January 1945, Allied forces started to advance east again toward Germany. This time, there would be no stopping them.

Chapter 10

ACTION IN THE PACIFIC

In late January 1945, Dickey Chapelle got accredited to the Pacific Fleet. She was ordered to report to the Naval Air Station in Oakland, California. There a young naval officer asked her where she wanted to go.

"Did he honestly mean I had a choice?" Chapelle wondered. "Very well, I'd make one. I'd tell the truth." So she told him, "As far forward as you'll let me."

Chapelle was born Georgette Louise Meyer and grew up in Milwaukee, Wisconsin. At the age of sixteen, Dickey, a math whiz, went to the Massachusetts Institute of Technology, but flunked out because she spent all her time hanging out at the local airport, learning all she could about aviation.

Soon, Dickey was writing articles about air shows and daredevil aviators. Before long, she had taken up photography and

When Dickey Chapelle received her accreditation, she took this photo of herself in a mirror, which is why the C appears reversed.

married her teacher, Tony Chapelle. Tony was a navy photographer, and although he opposed the idea, Dickey got accredited as a news photographer.

In early 1945, she told Ralph Daigh, the managing editor of Fawcett Publications, that she "wanted to cover what women were doing in the Pacific and anything else that happens while I'm out there."

"Go ahead," said Daigh. "Just be sure you're first someplace."

While Chapelle was making arrangements to go to the Pacific,

American forces invaded Iwo Jima, a small, barren volcanic island. Waves of marines charged ashore on beaches that were covered with ankle-deep black cinders and volcanic ash. Fighting against well-protected and heavily armed Japanese troops, the marines gained ground yard by yard.

Two days after the attack began, Bonnie Wiley, of AP, was on board a hospital ship just off the shore of Iwo Jima. Wiley had started her career in journalism right after she graduated from high school in Yakima, Washington. She got accredited in January 1945 and headed for the Pacific, where she knew there "was a big story breaking." Murlin Spencer, head of AP war correspondents, greeted her gruffly: "'Why did those (censored) editors send me a WOMAN correspondent!'" Wiley later discovered that Spencer's "bark was beautiful but his bite was toothless."

Wiley sent several dispatches from just off Iwo Jima, but her ship sailed before one of the most famous events of World War II happened—the raising of the American flag on Mount Suribachi, the highest point on Iwo Jima.

However, Patricia Lochridge, of *Woman's Home Companion,* was there aboard the hospital ship *Solace*. A graduate of the Columbia School of Journalism, Lochridge got her first job with a small newspaper in Mexico, Missouri. In the late 1930s, CBS in New York hired her to write news because she was willing to double as a secretary.

On board the *Solace,* Lochridge wrote, "The wounded came on and on. Some still had their rifles; others were naked except for their battle dressings. Most were in terrible pain. All were terribly brave." But then, very early one morning, a wounded marine arrived and half raised himself in his stretcher to look shoreward and exclaimed, "Take a look at that."

"And then we saw it," Lochridge wrote, "an American flag on the peak, snapping in the wind. The marine lay back and smiled. 'I helped put her there this morning,' he said."

While the battle for Iwo Jima raged, a group of nurses in Honolulu were flown to Guam, an island south of Iwo Jima. That was the first time American women in the armed forces were ordered to go beyond Hawaii. Dickey Chapelle was with them.

Shortly after she arrived in Guam, Chapelle was in the press room when the news of the flag raising on Iwo Jima came over the teletype. "The words galvanized the press room," she wrote. "Three of the men cheered. Now that I was sure it was all right for a correspondent to show emotion, I wiped my eyes with my knuckles. The Associated Press man...wiped his eyeglasses."

A navy lieutenant motioned Chapelle into his office and asked her where she wanted to go.

"I still couldn't imagine a correspondent making any other reply, but 'Iwo Jima,'" Chapelle recalled. "Nor could I imagine that the Navy would let me go. Forlornly I said, 'As far forward as you'll let me.'"

"Stay here, girl," the lieutenant told her as he left his office. In a few minutes, he returned with orders for Chapelle to board the hospital ship *Samaritan,* leaving for Iwo Jima at five o'clock the next morning.

That night, alone in her hilltop tent, Chapelle realized that there was no way to make arrangements to be woken up. Exhausted from her long airplane flight, she knew she could easily sleep for forty-eight hours.

"Well," she wrote, "there was exactly one way out. For nine hours in the dark and silence, I kept myself awake."

The *Samaritan*, like all hospital ships, was painted white with huge red crosses on either side. When it reached Iwo Jima, Chapelle took photos as load after load of critically wounded marines was placed on board—753 in all, hundreds more than it was built to carry.

"I still don't understand why lookers-on of battle try to use words to tell what they've seen. Or why I do. You don't remember

On board the U.S.S. Samaritan, *Dickey Chapelle took this photo of boats ferrying wounded soldiers from the beach on Iwo Jima to the hospital ship. Mount Suribachi is in the background.*

the things of war with the part of your being that forms and chooses words. It's not that the brain forgets," Chapelle later wrote. But, she continued, it was her stomach that remembered "how the ship smelled...the difference between the orthopedic wards where there always was plaster dust in the air from the fresh casts, and...the wards for abdominal injuries, where the smell was of decomposing flesh." Her ears remembered "the ceaseless surge of small boat engines beside us as they delivered their loads...the human noises...the curses and commands and breathing of the seamen carrying stretchers hour after hour. And how people sound when they are hurting terribly." Her feet

Dickey Chapelle photographed this critically wounded marine, Corporal Bill Fenton from Pennsylvania, on board the Samaritan. Fenton survived, and ten months later Chapelle visited him and his family on Christmas Day in a military hospital. Prior to the fall of 1943, military police censored any photograph of wounded or dead American soldiers. The ban was lifted because the military believed that pictures of bloodied soldiers would motivate Americans to continue supporting the war.

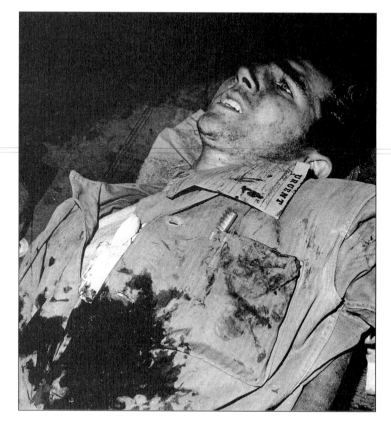

remembered the blood on the deck and "that it was slippery... and you had to be careful when you were standing in it not to fall down when the ship rolled."

But, Chapelle concluded, none of those "is as unfading as what the heart remembers... the eternal, incredible, appalling, macabre, irreverent, joyous gestures of love for life... made by the wounded."

On board the *Samaritan*, Chapelle took one of her most famous pictures of World War II. It was of a dying marine, Private First Class Johnny Hood from Waycross, Georgia. Only he did not die. Instead, he cheerfully greeted Chapelle a day later and told her that she had taken his picture the day before. She was sure she had not. But Hood insisted. Finally, Chapelle gave him her notebook, where she recorded the dog tag number of every man she had photographed. Quickly, he found his number.

A blood transfusion of fourteen pints had saved Johnny Hood's life. Chapelle took his picture again, and her before-and-after pictures of the "dying marine" were used by the Red Cross on posters to recruit blood donors for years after the war.

Chapelle got a second trip to Iwo Jima to photograph blood transfusions at a field hospital. Japanese snipers were still in the area, and when the pilot landed, he shouted at her, "Don't walk— *run!*" In the hospital, she photographed a mortally wounded marine who insisted on giving her his eight-inch-long, double-edged trench knife in a sheath. "Here, you take it," he told her. "Where I'm going, I won't need one. And if you ever do, you'll need it bad."

Before she left Iwo Jima, Chapelle asked some officers to take her to the front lines. After a forty-minute drive, they stopped. Seeing nothing of interest, Chapelle set off by herself to a nearby

Dickey Chapelle made two trips to Iwo Jima. She took many photos, including this one of a field hospital during the first quiet period since the battle began. In the foreground, three navy doctors are taking a break.

ridge. There was not much to see from the top, but she took photos anyway, all the while hearing the "noise of bugs" whizzing by. When she returned, the officers could not believe she had been so stupid as to stand up like that. "Do you realize—all the artillery and half the snipers on *both* sides of this [expletive deleted] war had ten full minutes to make up their minds about you," one shouted.

That night back on Guam, Chapelle told her story to Barbara Finch, of Reuters News Service. When she got to the part about the whizzing bugs, Finch said, "There were what?"

"Wasps, I guess. Insect noises, anyhow," Chapelle answered.

"I guess somebody will have to tell you," Finch replied. "There is no insect life on Iwo Jima. It's a dead volcano."

In a squeaking voice, Chapelle said, "You mean, those weren't—"

"They were not wasps," Finch said with certainty.

Finally, Chapelle realized. Those had been bullets whizzing by.

On her dispatch for that day, she typed: "Dateline: March 5, 1945, Iwo Jima. Under Fire."

On April 1, American forces invaded Okinawa. Dickey Chapelle was with the invasion force on board the hospital ship *Relief*. Her orders were to take more blood-transfusion pictures.

Eventually, the fighting would be the bloodiest yet. But at first, the Americans easily occupied three-fourths of the island. With no casualties on the *Relief* needing blood transfusions, Chapelle got navy permission to go ashore to photograph the delivery of blood to an army field hospital on Brown Beach. But the surf was too high at Brown Beach, and the amphibious tractor dropped her off at Orange Beach.

"I won't be back for you today," the driver shouted as he left. "The wind's coming up."

Although under strict orders to return that night, Chapelle was stranded. Two marines gave her a bone-rattling ride through dangerous territory to marine headquarters. When the commander saw her, he told the marines, "Get that broad the hell out of here."

The marines took her to the marine press camp, where the welcome was only slightly warmer. That night kamikaze attacks began. These were attacks by planes loaded with explosives flown by pilots who would make suicide crashes. But first, they strafed the area. The noise, Chapelle later recalled, was deafening.

Kamikaze attacks, snipers, and bad weather kept Chapelle on Okinawa for days. Throughout it all, she traveled to marine field hospitals to take photos. One night while a surgeon operated on a

At a cemetery on Guam, Dickey Chapelle took this photo of the burial of an American soldier, who died from wounds during the battle of Iwo Jima.

marine, she held a flashlight for two hours with the beam pointed straight down so the "glow wouldn't tempt an enemy sniper."

Chapelle did not know it, but the navy had issued an arrest-on-sight order for her because she had "jumped ship." The marines knew, but they ignored the order because they liked Chapelle. Besides, her photos would show the marines in action to the folks back home.

On the sixth day, a marine finally told Chapelle about the order. The original order, he said, had come through as "shoot on sight."

Chapelle turned herself in and was arrested, evacuated from Okinawa, and put on a ship just as the Japanese launched their deadliest kamikaze attack and sank twenty ships. Her ship survived, and she was taken back to Guam. There a marine took her at gunpoint to an airport, where he turned her over to a navy flight nurse for a ride home with a planeload of wounded men.

"'You got her now?'" the stern-faced marine asked the nurse.

"'We got her. She's been delivered into the navy's hands, marine.'"

The marine holstered his gun, looked straight at Chapelle, and gave her a big grin.

"'So long, Dickey. Whatever it is, you tell 'em you didn't do it!'"

Chapelle was disaccredited and, although she tried, unable to get reaccredited. Her editor tried, too. "It is our considered opinion," he wrote to the navy, "that the decision to discipline Mrs. Chapelle was made largely because of her sex."

CHICAGO DAILY NEWS

WARMER
Fair and mild today and Friday. Clear and
rather cold tonight. Low tonight 38. Sunrise
7:16. Sunset 6:49.

70TH YEAR—57. *SEC. U.S. PAT. OFF. COPYRIGHT, 1945 BY THE CHICAGO DAILY NEWS, INC.*   THURSDAY, MARCH 8, 1945—THIRTY-TWO PAGES.   *Telephone DEarborn 1111.*   FOUR CENTS

RED STREAK

Rundstedt's Worst Licking Since D-Day

WE'RE OVER RHINE

1st Army Troops Streaming Over River

Chapter 11

CROSSING THE RHINE

Dickey Chapelle had gone as far forward as the navy would let her, and beyond. Now, for her, the war was over.

The war was not over, however, for other women correspondents.

In Europe in early 1945, Allied forces were fighting their way across German-occupied France toward Germany. Lee Miller had managed to get a jeep and was moving with Allied soldiers as they fought to free one town after another in the Alsace region. "Pheasants and partridges and the tiny deer were so used to small-arms fire and the thunder of guns that they didn't take fright when they were shot at themselves," Miller wrote of the countryside there.

Miller photographed soldiers "making a fabulous stew in an old water bucket" from the leg of a shell-killed cow, and other soldiers sleeping on bags of flour in a bombed-out mill. She photographed soldiers being decorated for field bravery, German prisoners, burned-out tanks, and devastated cities.

Sonia Tomara was also in Alsace with the American Seventh Army. One afternoon, a guide took Tomara and several other correspondents to the top of a mountain covered with fir trees. It was cold and snowing. There they toured Struthof, a small concentration camp. Refugees had been relating chilling stories about such death camps, but now, for the first time, some correspondents actually saw one and its gas chamber and realized how true the stories were.

Iris Carpenter and Lee Carson traveled with the First Army as it moved into Germany and headed toward Cologne, a major river port on the Rhine River. The Rhine, Germany's most vital waterway, was the last major obstacle between the Allies and the heart of Germany.

Toni Frissell photographed this child, whose parents had died in a bombing raid, holding his teddy bear. She reported, "The worst part of war, in my opinion, is what happens to the survivors—the widows without home or family, the ragged kids left to wander as orphans. The aftereffects of war are never pretty to see. Neither should they be forgotten."

On the way to Cologne, Carpenter reported, "Every road was an unending column of tanks and supply vehicles. The shattering din of the tracks and wheels was enough to make the head spin—without the crashing of guns." The weather was "bitterly cold, with the wet raw cold that nothing would keep out."

Allied bombers had dropped forty-two thousand tons of bombs on Cologne, the third-largest city in Germany. When the First Army arrived, Carpenter described Cologne as the "third largest rubble pile" in Germany.

The retreating German army had blown up bridges across the Rhine. However, two days later, a patrol of the First Army discovered that the Ludendorff railway bridge in the town of Remagen was still intact.

The patrol captured the town but soon learned that the railroad bridge had been wired with explosives that were set to go off at four o'clock. In the face of German machine-gun fire, a team of army engineers managed to cut and shoot through the wires just minutes before four.

The next day, Iris Carpenter drove to the bridge with Stanley and Mac, two male correspondents, and Shanks, their favorite jeep driver. They arrived caked with mud after seven dangerous hours in miserable weather. They had to leave their jeep and "foot it" with the infantry across the planks that had been laid over the railroad tracks. An MP told them to "keep ten paces between you and the next guy—it's hot around here!"

Despite the shaky footing and the realization that they were easy targets for German snipers, Carpenter could not help noticing "the incredible loveliness of the Rhineland....There were terraced vineyards, and cream and yellow villages looking like bunches of primroses tucked into the country's corsage." But

Lee Miller photographed troops wearing camouflage to blend in with the snow during the bitterly cold winter of 1945 in the Alsace region of France.

then, she reported, "there was Stanley looking back and saying, 'Don't look at his face, Iris,' as we had to step over the body of a fair-haired German boy in the narrow footpath above the steely gray and swiftly flowing river (does it ever, I wonder, look as blue as that German boy's eyes?)."

Once the Allies crossed the Rhine, Carpenter wrote, "the great-est story of the war—the story of the final Nazi break-up—started to move so fast there was no keeping up with it."

One day, Carpenter decided to see the scene from a Piper Cub plane. The panoramic view was terrific, and she got a great story— but only after flying for three hours in a storm, getting lost for an hour over enemy territory, and landing with "no more gas left than would have filled a cigarette lighter."

The Allies moved through Germany "blitz-bashing every vil-lage until there was nothing left of it but a feeling of resentment on the part of the folks who wouldn't be able to live there anymore." The displaced villagers were among the hordes of refugees in Germany. These included people who were being freed from Nazi prisons and people who had been enslaved to work on farms and in factories, including Poles, Czechs, Russians, French, Dutch, Norwegians, and Danes. For one group of refugees who were packed into a church almost to the point of being suffocated, Carpenter reported, "there was no sanitation, no water, no food, no hope."

In April 1945, Allied forces started large-scale liberation of con-centration camps. "We thought we had seen the ultimate in horror, suffering, and misery," Carpenter wrote. "That was before we got deeply enough into Germany to overrun the concentration camps."

For years, refugees had told stories about the camps. But Carpenter, like many other people, doubted that things were "as bad as people had said they were." Or if such camps did exist, "they must be merely isolated instances of sadism not reflective of Nazi policy in general."

The Lager Dora camp, near Nordhausen in central Germany,

was the first camp Carpenter entered. After seeing it, her doubts disappeared. "Well," she wrote, "we knew differently now."

The stench, she wrote, turned her and her companions as "green as the trees." Words were not adequate to truly describe the sight of people in the final stages of starvation who lay crowded together on tiers of wood bunks, or the emaciated naked bodies of dead people heaped up in a pile of tangled legs and arms.

On April 10, Allied troops entered Buchenwald, the first major camp to be liberated. The next day, Marguerite Higgins, a new war correspondent, arrived there.

Marguerite Higgins preparing to type a dispatch while in Germany in 1945.

Higgins was born in Hong Kong and grew up in Oakland, California. The biggest problem she faced as a correspondent, she said, was the "tendency of some male officials to associate the combination of femininity and blond hair with either dumbness or slyness, or both."

Higgins arrived at Buchenwald thinking that the story of the ovens might be "exposed as fabrications"—until she was shown the oven rooms and the bodies, thousands of bodies—stacks of bodies, jumbled heaps of bodies, bodies piled on carts, and bodies propped against buildings. "As if to emphasize the horror," she reported, "the frosty spring nights had frozen into ghastly stalactites the trickles of blood and yellow bubbles of mucus that oozed from the eyes and nose of the many who had been bludgeoned or otherwise tortured to death."

Margaret Bourke-White was also among the first to arrive at Buchenwald. Immediately, she started taking pictures. "Even though I did not realize how soon people would disbelieve or forget," she later wrote, "I had a deep conviction that an atrocity like this demanded to be recorded. So I forced myself to map the place with negatives."

Lee Miller took pictures at Buchenwald and cabled her editor at *Vogue:* "I IMPLORE YOU TO BELIEVE THIS IS TRUE." Miller's graphic pictures appeared in both the British and the American editions of *Vogue* under the headline "Believe It."

Shortly after Buchenwald, Bourke-White, Lee Carson, two male correspondents, and a soldier made a chilling discovery. They had set off in search of an aircraft small-parts factory. On the way, they began to smell a peculiar odor and soon stumbled upon a burned-out area covered with bones. Then they saw charred human bodies along a barbed-wire fence. "We stood frozen with

At the Buchenwald concentration camp, Margaret Bourke-White photographed these German citizens being forced to walk past piles of corpses to see what their Nazi leaders had done.

horror," Carson reported. Bourke-White sobbed while she took pictures. One of the men threw up.

Soon several skeletal survivors emerged from a nearby woods and told the story of the Erla work camp. The 350 Erla prisoners worked in an aircraft factory. Learning that American troops were closing in, the guards used big vats of soup to lure the starving prisoners into the wooden barracks. Then the guards barred the doors and windows, poured flammable liquid on the building, and set it ablaze. The charred bodies were all that remained of the few men who had managed to break out of the burning building before they died. The survivors had been outside the barracks when the fire started.

Allied authorities had known the location of many camps long before they were liberated, but the first they knew of Erla came from Bourke-White, Carson, and their colleagues.

THE MILWAUKEE JOURNAL

Sixty-third Year | Circulation Yesterday .....317,410 ♦ Circulation One Year Ago..312,190 | Monday, May 7, 1945 | Daily ....3 Cents Sunday ....10 Cents | Four Pages

Copyright, 1945, by The Journal Company

All Germans Surrender to Three Major Allies

Chapter 12

WINNING THE WAR

As Allied forces advanced east across Germany, Soviet forces advanced west. A linkup between the two mighty forces was to take place at the town of Torgau, on the east side of the Elbe River. For many people, the linkup would be the climactic event of the war. As the armies approached, hundreds of correspondents headed toward Torgau.

Ann Stringer, of the United Press, got there first.

Stringer grew up in Texas and never hesitated to say, "I can write the pants off of any man." Stringer's husband, Bill, also of UP, had been killed on D-Day. Still grieving, she got herself attached to the Ninth Army as it moved toward Germany. Some of her colleagues feared that her move was really a "death wish." On the contrary, Stringer explained, "I preferred to stay alive and get the story."

Stringer was supposed to be on her way back to Paris. SHAEF

*Ann Stringer
interviewing American
soldiers in Germany
in 1945.*

had ordered her back because she had been caught going too far forward. Instead, she hooked up with Allan Jackson, an INS photographer who had an old Ford automobile. On April 25, Stringer and Jackson convinced two pilots to take them up in their Piper Cubs to look for the approaching Russians. While in the air, Stringer heard voices talking in Russian coming over her plane's radio. The planes landed in a clover field near Torgau. Stringer, Jackson, and the pilots climbed over two army roadblocks and walked to Torgau.

There, suddenly, Stringer saw a young man running toward them. He wore only blue shorts and a gray cap with a red hammer

Reds Swim Elbe, Hail 'Americanskis'

By ANN STRINGER,
United Press War Correspondent.

TORGAU Germany, April 26 (Delayed).—Down the street of Torgau came a Russian youth wearing blue shorts and a gray cap with a red hammer and sickle on it.

"Bravo, Americanski!" he yelled. "Bravo comrades!"

He was dripping wet because he had swum the Elde River to greet us. It was my first glimpse of the Russian Army.

Ann Stringer.

I had just flown in a Piper Cub plane into this historic town where the official juncture of the Americans and Russians took place. We landed in a clover field, climbed over two road blocks and then saw the young Russian running up the

Texas. The Russian soldiers insisted that we meet the commander of their regiment, so we started off. I noticed that almost all of our escort wore at least one brilliantly colored metal on their greenish tunics.

We were introduced to the commander, a quiet, stocky man with jet black hair. We gave the Russians our autographs. They gave us theirs. The commander invited us to lunch.

Ann Stringer's dispatch ran on the front page of the New York World-Telegram.

and sickle on it. "He was dripping wet," Stringer reported, "because he had swum the Elbe River to greet us.

"'Bravo, Americanski!' the Russian soldier yelled. 'Bravo, comrades!'" Together, they crossed the Elbe in an old canoe and met the Soviet regimental commander. Everyone exchanged autographs and then sat down to lunch, which included many toasts.

Confident that she was the first reporter to witness the arrival of the Russians, Stringer knew that she had a major scoop. Now she had to figure out how to file her story in Paris.

Jackson gave her his film and went to reclaim his car. Stringer tried to talk her pilot into flying her to Paris. He refused. He could only fly toward the east. Not knowing what else to do, Stringer climbed into the plane and headed away from Paris. Then, suddenly, her pilot spotted an American C-47 on the ground and landed beside it.

The C-47 was leaving shortly for Paris, but the pilots refused to take Stringer. "I just met the Russians," she told them. They didn't believe her.

So she pulled out her typewriter, sat down on the wing of their plane, and started typing her story, in which she included the names of the C-47 pilots. That convinced them, and Stringer had her ride to Paris.

From the airport outside Paris, Stringer hitchhiked to press headquarters at the Hotel Scribe. She filed her story and delivered Jackson's film to the censors. Exhausted, she went to the press bar, where she bumped into a correspondent for the *New York Times*. He was stunned to see her back. She was missing the big story at Torgau, he told her. Stringer merely smiled. He would find out soon enough that she had scooped them all.

Stringer's story made the headlines across the United States. Her scoop infuriated many of her colleagues in the U.S. First Army press camp. Iris Carpenter, however, who had had many scoops herself, said, "She did it, bless her heart."

A few days later, Marguerite Higgins got a scoop for which she would be awarded a journalism prize for getting the story that involved the greatest risk. She also was awarded an army campaign ribbon for outstanding service with the armed forces under difficult conditions.

Higgins had teamed up with Sergeant Peter Furst, a corre-

Lee Miller (seated in center) in Torgau, Germany, with Russian women soldiers.

spondent for *Stars and Stripes*. Furst had a jeep, and he and Higgins headed for Dachau after they heard rumors that American troops were about to free the huge concentration camp there. On the way, they learned that about seven miles of road ahead of them were still under German control. As they were deciding whether to proceed, the driver of a larger military vehicle volunteered to lead the way.

They passed villages draped with white flags, and some Germans even cheered them. Bedraggled German soldiers wanted to surrender to them. "We disarmed Germans until our jeep could hold no more weapons," Higgins reported. Anxious about having loaded weapons around, she was "especially uneasy about the German grenades clunking about in the back of the jeep."

When Higgins and Furst arrived in the town of Dachau, they learned that fighting was going on at the northern outskirts of the camp. But, some Germans told them, white flags had been seen at the southern end, by the main administration buildings. Detouring around the fighting, Higgins and Furst headed for the southern end. They arrived to find an SS general "staggering under a huge white flag."

Higgins and Furst asked the general to assign an SS officer to take them to the electrically charged barbed-wire enclosure where

Iris Carpenter interviewing American soldiers in Torgau.

the prisoners were kept. To get to the prison enclosure, they had to cross an area guarded by heavily armed SS men in watchtowers. These guards might or might not be ready to surrender.

Just short of the watchtower area, Furst stopped the jeep. Higgins got out to reconnoiter on foot. About to cross an open stretch, Higgins heard Furst shouting and pointing. Looking up, she saw a watchtower crammed with SS men. "Rifles were at the ready and the machine gun was trained on me," Higgins wrote. Though she had no idea what prompted her, she ignored Furst's frantic motions for her to retreat. Instead, she shouted to the guards: *"Kommen Sie hier, bitte. Wir sind Amerikaner"* [Come here, please. We are Americans].

The guards came and surrendered their weapons. Furst put the

Toni Frissell with an officer on the Siegfried Line, the Allies' name for a thirty-five-mile-long defensive barrier that Germany built on its western frontier. She is setting up her camera tripod among the concrete "teeth" built to prevent tanks from crossing the terrain. The heavily fortified line also included many minefields, fortresses, and concrete bunkers.

Women correspondents had to scramble to get transportation. Ruth Cowan staked out this jeep in 1944.

SS officer on the hood of their jeep, handed Higgins a cocked pistol, and drove to the prisoners' area. The prisoners were in their barracks, "tensely waiting" to find out if they had been liberated.

"Sie sind frei. Sie sind frei. Die Amerikaner sind hier" [You are free. You are free. The Americans are here], Higgins and Furst shouted.

The prisoners rushed out of their barracks. "I have never seen such wild joy and pandemonium," Higgins wrote. The prisoners had no idea that she was a woman, Higgins reported, because "there were no conventional guides to recognition, for I had on a fur-lined hat with fur ear flaps, fatigue pants, and shirt." On top of that she wore a bulky, fur-lined German army jacket that she had "liberated" from a German warehouse. For half an hour, the prisoners carried Higgins and Furst around on their shoulders. They were even "tossed from shoulder to shoulder." Both of them, Higgins reported, "got badly bruised" in that "wild first half hour."

When American troops arrived, a general grabbed Higgins and roughly dragged her out of the enclosure.

"'What the hell are you doing in there?'" the general shouted. "'Don't you know the place is raging with typhus?'"

The general shook Higgins so hard that it took her breath away. Then she found her voice and shouted back.

"'God damnit to hell! Lay off. You let go of me. I've had my typhus shot. I'm in here doing my job.'"

That same general later recommended Higgins for the army campaign ribbon.

Martha Gellhorn had first heard about Dachau in 1937, when she was covering the Spanish civil war. She heard about it from a German who had fled Germany. Now, in 1945, several days after Dachau was liberated, she arrived. By then medical facilities had been set up, the buildings had been scrubbed clean, and nurses were living in the houses where the SS guards had lived. For several days, she toured the place and interviewed former prisoners.

Gellhorn was at Dachau the day Germany surrendered to the Allies, May 7, 1945. "Dachau seemed to me," she wrote, "the most suitable place in Europe to hear the news of victory. For surely this war was made to abolish Dachau, and all the other places like Dachau, and everything that Dachau stood for, and to abolish it forever."

In August, the United States dropped two atomic bombs on Japan. The bombs created a heat wave that incinerated thousands of people. At least 130,000 people died immediately or within a few hours. Thousands more suffered severe burns and radiation sickness.

On August 14, Japan surrendered.

Finally, World War II was over.

Marguerite Higgins's dispatch from Dachau in the New York Herald Tribune.

33,000 Dachau Captives Freed By 7th Army

110.000 Are Liberated at Moosburg; Nazi Doctor Admits Killing 21,000

By Marguerite Higgins

By Wireless to the Herald Tribune
Copyright, 1945. New York Tribune Inc.

DACHAU, Germany. April 29 (Delayed).—Troops of the United States 7th Army liberated 33,000 prisoners this afternoon at this first and largest of the Nazi concentration camps. Some of the prisoners had endured for eleven years the horrors of notorious Dachau.

The liberation was a frenzied scene. Inmates of the camp hugged and embraced the American troops, kissed the ground before them and carried them shoulder high around the place.

[At Moosburg, north of Munich, the United States 14th Armored Division liberated 110,000 Allied prisoners of war, including 11,000 Americans, from Stalag 7A.

[From United States 12th Army Group headquarters came the story of a captured Nazi doctor, Gustav Wilhelm Schuebbe, who said that the Nazi annihilation institute at (Continued on page 4, column 3)

"There are so many things to think about when you are coming home after a war," wrote Martha Gellhorn. "You think in small amazed snatches, saying to yourself, how in God's name did they get all those ships there on D-Day…and how did anyone survive Italy?"

Martha Gellhorn returned home to America with a planeload of wounded soldiers. The plane was "full of nice people even though it smelled pretty awful the way wounds and bodies and drainage bottles will smell; and it was a happy plane. I couldn't even imagine what home would be like because home was written on everyone's face so lovingly, so hopefully; home must be the end of the rainbow. Then we landed late at night at Mitchel Field and everyone was silent when the doors opened and the hot air of American summer came in."

Toni Frissell photographed this American soldier in Italy on Easter Sunday, 1945. She reported, "We went to a green hill covered with flowers: hyacinth, yellow and pink primroses. One man was carefully decorating camouflage on his tin hat with flowers stuck in the netting mesh. What an Easter bonnet."

Chapter 13

AFTER THE WAR

Jobs in journalism got scarce for women as men returned from the military. Now that the war was won, the prevailing attitude in America was that women should devote themselves to their husband and children. By 1968, there would be fewer women foreign correspondents than there had been in the prewar years. It took new laws and regulations, spurred by the feminist movement of the 1970s, to open doors for women in journalism. It was a slow process until the late 1990s, when there was a dramatic increase in the number of women entering the field.

In the aftermath of World War II, Martha Gellhorn wondered how people would adjust. "For the war," she wrote, "the hated and perilous and mad, had been home for a long time too; everyone had learned how to live in it, everyone had something to do, something that looked necessary, and now we were back in this beautiful big safe place called home and what would become of us?"

Each woman war correspondent answered that question differently. Here is an abbreviated fast-forward through their postwar lives:

Margaret Bourke-White continued to chronicle dramatic global events. She went to India and took one of her most famous photographs, "Gandhi at His Spinning Wheel." She photographed life under apartheid in South Africa. While photographing the Korean War in the mid-1950s, she discovered that she had Parkinson's disease. Eventually the disease curtailed her activities, but she still managed to write her autobiography. She died in 1971. Bourke-White left a legacy of memorable picture essays, books, and classic photographs that may be found in many museum collections.

Margaret Bourke-White in the cockpit of a B-47, a new, fast, all-jet bomber built after the war. She was on postwar assignment to do a story for Life *on the Strategic Air Command.*

Iris Carpenter came to the United States on a ship, carrying only her typewriter and duffel bags. She became a U.S. citizen and married an officer from the First Army, whom she later divorced. She wrote a book about her war experiences, worked for the *Boston Globe,* and produced a radio show, *World Opinion Roundup,* for the Voice of America.

Lee Carson returned from covering the war wearing her paratrooper's boots, GI pants, and Eisenhower jacket. "She was fresh from the fighting fronts; excited, voluble, more than a little tired, but full of the adventures," her boss at INS recalled. During the next two decades, she wrote for magazines and married twice. She died of cancer at a young age.

Toni Frissell showing her camera to children in England in March 1945. After the war, Frissell devoted herself to photographing a wide range of subjects, including the Berlin Wall in Germany, national political conventions in the United States, and the wedding of John and Jacqueline Kennedy. In 1970, she donated her extraordinary and massive collection of photographs, negatives, and manuscripts to the Library of Congress.

Dickey Chapelle's favorite picture of herself, taken in 1959 by M/Sgt. Lew Lowery, whom she met during the battle for Iwo Jima.

Dickey Chapelle kept on taking risks to cover hot spots around the world—the Hungarian Revolution, the Algerians' fight for independence, and the Vietnam War. She made thirty parachute jumps with the troops in Vietnam. In 1965, Dickey Chapelle stepped on a land mine there and was killed. At the time, she had a small white flower in her helmet and was wearing tiny pearl earrings. Her last words were reported to be, "I guess it was bound to happen." In a tribute by the Women's National Press Club, Chapelle was honored as a journalist who "was always where the action was."

Ruth Cowan was elected president of the Women's National Press Club. A Washington correspondent for the AP, she resigned at the age of fifty-one, perhaps because she knew that the AP did not look kindly on women over the age of fifty-five. She was appointed to a government post by President Eisenhower.

Virginia Cowles was a roving reporter for the *Sunday Times* of London. She received the Order of the British Empire for her war reporting. Shortly after the war, she coauthored a play with Martha Gellhorn about two women war correspondents. She married a man who had been in a German prisoner-of-war camp, raised three children, and wrote biographies.

Lyn Crost wrote *Honor by Fire,* the first book about the Nisei soldiers in World War II. Her typewriter, war uniform, and trench coat are in a display about the Nisei soldiers at the Smithsonian Institution's National Museum of American History.

Martha Gellhorn divorced Ernest Hemingway, adopted an Italian war orphan, and covered wars until she was in her eighties. She published novels, novellas, collections of short stories, collections of her war correspondence and peacetime articles, and a travel memoir. "Reading Martha Gellhorn for the first time is a staggering experience....She is...one of the most eloquent witnesses of the 20th century," wrote Bill Buford, fiction editor of *The New Yorker*.

Marguerite Higgins covered the Korean War and risked her life several times. She won a Pulitzer Prize for her coverage of combat. She got married, had three children, and continued her career. She was eight months pregnant when she covered President

Richard Nixon's trip to the Soviet Union. Her twenty-two-year career with the *Herald Tribune* ended when she started expressing her opposition to U.S. policy in Vietnam. During one of her many trips to Vietnam, she contracted a rare tropical disease. She knew that the disease was fatal. In the months before her death, at the age of forty-five, she continued to write a column for *Newsday* from her hospital bed.

Marguerite Higgins typing a dispatch during the Korean War. Her face has camouflage paint on it.

Peggy Hull Deuell (her married name), who began covering the American military in 1916 (see photo on page ix), was told that she was too old to cover World War II. But she persisted and finally got accredited to cover the war in the Pacific theater for the Cleveland Plain Dealer. *In appreciation of her presence, soldiers gave her patches that represented their particular unit. By the time the war ended, she had eight berets with fifty patches. She retired to the Carmel Valley in California and lived there until her death in 1967.*

Helen Kirkpatrick worked as a roving European correspondent for the *New York Post* for a few years. She covered world events in Moscow, India, Pakistan, Afghanistan, and Turkey. She quit in a dispute over editorial policy and became chief of information for an agency of the French government. For her wartime and postwar work, she won the French Légion d'Honneur, the French Médaille de la Reconnaissance, and the U.S. Medal of Freedom.

Patricia Lochridge had a career as a hard-hitting journalist. She wrote exposés of the trucking industry and the black market in

New Orleans. Eventually, she moved to Hawaii and lectured for many years at the University of Hawaii.

Lee Miller traveled in Europe and photographed the aftermath of the war. Then she got married and had a baby. Her son, Antony, later recalled that while he was growing up, Miller "almost never talked about the war." Once, however, he told her that he had heard in school that the Americans had made up the story of the concentration camps as a "smear campaign" against the Nazis. She did not say much, he recalled, but "the cold hardness which entered her voice when she spoke...authenticated her statement beyond doubt." After her death, Antony established the Lee Miller Archives in England.

Inez Robb had a long, productive career as a journalist and received many awards for her columns and articles. "I love my work," she wrote. "I guess I was just born to be a newspaper woman."

Sigrid Schultz covered the Nuremberg war crimes trials after the war. Then she worked as a commentator for the Mutual Broadcasting System. In time, she criticized war correspondents, who she thought had become nothing more than cheerleaders for the military. In 1969, the Overseas Press Club presented her with a plaque that was inscribed in part, "To a tough competitor, staunch friend, honest reporter."

Ann Stringer covered postwar events in Europe and continued getting scoops until 1949. Then she remarried and devoted herself to building her husband's career as a photographer. After thirty mostly unhappy years, she got divorced and resumed writing. "Develop your own talents. Make your own way," she told young women. "No one can take that from you."

Sonia Tomara was in her late forties when the war ended. Resigning from the *Herald Tribune,* she married William Clark, who became a federal judge. In 1948, Clark was hired to reform the German courts, and they lived in Germany for seven years. Clark died in 1957. For the rest of her life, Sonia Tomara lived with her sister Irina in Princeton, New Jersey. She was working on her memoirs when she died, at the age of eighty-five.

Betty Wason wrote twenty-three books and had a long career in radio broadcasting.

Bonnie Wiley went to college and graduate school and taught journalism in various universities. In explaining why she did not cover the Korean War, Wiley said, "One war to cover in a lifetime is enough—maybe too much."

SELECTED BIBLIOGRAPHY

Books by Women War Correspondents

Bonney, Thérèse. *Europe's Children.* New York: Plantin Press, 1943.

Bourke-White, Margaret. *Portrait of Myself.* New York: Simon & Schuster, 1963.

　　Shooting the Russian War. New York: Simon & Schuster, 1942.

　　They Called It "Purple Heart Valley." New York: Simon & Schuster, 1944.

Carpenter, Iris. *No Woman's World.* Boston: Houghton Mifflin, 1946.

Chapelle, Dickey. *What's a Woman Doing Here? (A Reporter's Report on Herself).* New York: William R. Morrow, 1962.

Cowles, Virginia. *Looking for Trouble.* New York: Harper & Brothers, 1941.

Crost, Lyn. *Honor by Fire: Japanese Americans at War in Europe and the Pacific.* Novato, CA: Presidio Press, 1994.

Gellhorn, Martha. *The Face of War.* New York: Atlantic Monthly Press, 1988.

Higgins, Marguerite. *News Is a Singular Thing.* Garden City, NY: Doubleday, 1955.

Kirkpatrick, Helen. *This Terrible Peace.* London: Rich & Cowan, 1938.

Rinehart, Mary Roberts. *My Story.* New York: Rhinehart & Co., 1948.

Robb, Inez. *Don't Just Stand There.* New York: David McKay, 1962.

Stringer, Ann, and Henry Ries. *German Faces.* New York: William Sloane Associates, 1950.

Wason, Betty. *Miracle in Hellas.* New York: Macmillan, 1943.

Other Books

Beasley, Maurine H., and Sheila Gibbons. *Women in Media: A Documentary Source Book.* Washington, DC: Women's Institute for Freedom of the Press, 1977.

Callahan, Sean, ed. *The Photographs of Margaret Bourke-White.* New York: New York Graphic Society, 1972.

Edwards, Julia. *Women of the World: The Great Foreign Correspondents.* Boston: Houghton Mifflin, 1988.

Goldberg, Vicki. *Margaret Bourke-White.* Mankato, MN: Creative Education, 1980.

Kroeger, Brooke. *Nellie Bly.* New York: Times Books, 1994.

Matthews, Joseph J. *Reporting the Wars.* Minneapolis: University of Minnesota Press, 1957.

Oestreicher, J. C. *The World Is Their Beat.* New York: Duell, Sloan & Pearce, 1945.

Oldfield, Colonel Barney. *Never a Shot in Anger.* New York: Duell, Sloan & Pearce, 1956.

Penrose, Antony, ed. *Lee Miller's War: Photographer and Correspondent with the Allies in Europe 1944–45.* Boston: Little, Brown & Company, 1992.

Rollyson, Carl. *Nothing Ever Happens to the Brave: The Story of Martha Gellhorn.* New York: St. Martin's Press, 1990.

Schilpp, Madelon G., and Sharon M. Murphy. *Great Women of the Press.* Carbondale, IL: Southern Illinois University Press, 1983.

Smith, Wilda M., and Eleanor A. Bogart. *The Wars of Peggy Hull: The Life and Times of a War Correspondent.* El Paso, TX: Texas Western Press, 1991.

Sorel, Nancy Caldwell. *The Women Who Wrote the War.* New York: Arcade Publishing, 1999.

Toni Frissell: Photographs, 1933–1967. New York: Doubleday, 1994.

Voss, Frederick S. *Reporting the War: The Journalistic Coverage of World War II.* Washington, DC: Smithsonian Institution Press, 1994.

Wagner, Lilya. *Women War Correspondents of World War II.* Westport, CT: Greenwood Publishing, 1989.

Articles

Bourke-White, Margaret. "Czech Soldier." *Life* (October 3, 1938): cover.
    "Muscovites Take Up Their Guns as Nazi Horde Approaches." *Life* (October 27, 1941): 27–33.
    "Tunis Bombing: *Life* Photographer Margaret Bourke-White Accompanies Bombing Mission." *Life* (March 1, 1942): 17–23.
    "Women in Lifeboats." *Life* (February 22, 1943): 48–54.

Carpenter, Iris. "Globe Writer Recalls Her Greatest Thrill." *Boston Globe* (December 9, 1948).

Carson, Lee. "Bridgehead Becomes Hot Shooting Gallery." *New York Journal-American* (March 11, 1945).
    "Nazi Massacre of War Slaves." *New York Journal-American* (April 23, 1945).

Cowan, Ruth. "I Never Thought Women Could Live a Life So Hard." *St. Louis Post-Dispatch* (February 21, 1943).

Crost, Lyn. "Moving Fast, Taking Town, All in a Day's Work for Hawaii Soldiers." *Honolulu Star-Bulletin* (April 20, 1945).

Deuell, Peggy Hull. "V-E Day No Fiesta." *Cleveland Plain Dealer* (May 21, 1945).

Gellhorn, Martha. "Come Ahead, Adolf." *Collier's* (August 6, 1938): 13, 43–44.
    "Dachau: Experimental Murder." *Collier's* (June 23, 1945): 16ff. Reprinted in Martha Gellhorn, *The Faces of War.*
    "Death of a Dutch Town." *Collier's* (December 23, 1944): 21, 58–59. Reprinted as "A Little Dutch Town" in *The Faces of War.*
    "Obituary for a Democracy." *Collier's* (December 10, 1938): 12–13, 28–29. Reprinted in *The Faces of War.*
    "Only the Shells Whine." *Collier's* (July 17, 1937): 12–13, 64–65. Reprinted as

"High Explosives for Everyone" in *The Faces of War.*

"Visit Italy." *Collier's* (May 6, 1944): 62ff. Reprinted in *The Faces of War.*

"The Wounded Come Home." *Collier's* (August 5, 1944): 14–15, 73–74.

"The Wounds of Paris." *Collier's* (November 4, 1944): 12, 70.

"You're on Your Way Home." *Collier's* (September 22, 1945): 22, 39.

Higgins, Marguerite. "33,000 Dachau Captives Freed by 7th Army." *New York Herald Tribune* (May 1, 1945).

Kirkpatrick, Helen. "Air War Was like a Prize Fight, Observer Finds." *Chicago Daily News* (August 17, 1940).

"London Still Stood This Morning." *Chicago Daily News* (September 9, 1940).

Lockridge, Patricia. "Solace at Iwo." *Woman's Home Companion* (May 1945): 4ff.

Miller, Lee. "Report from France: The Fall of St. Malo." *Vogue* (October 1944): 92–93, 129–34, 136–37, 143.

"Believe It!" *Vogue* (June 1945): 104–07.

"Report from France: The Liberation of Paris." *Vogue* (November 1944): 94–95, 99, 147–50, 155.

"Through the Alsace Campaign." *Vogue* (May 1945): 140–43, 197.

Schultz, Sigrid. "Hitler Gazes at Stars to Guide His Decisions." *Chicago Tribune* (July 13, 1939).

Stringer, Ann. "Reds Swim Elbe, Hail 'Americanskis.'" *New York World-Telegram* (April 26, 1945).

Tomara, Sonia. "Nazis Cremated 1,665 Women at Camp in Alsace." *New York Herald Tribune* (December 10, 1944).

"Reporter with Paris Refugees Describes Nightmare Flight." *New York Herald Tribune* (June 15, 1940).

"Sonia Tomara Flies in a Raid over Hankow." *New York Herald Tribune* (August 24, 1943).

"Two News Women Honored for Work." *New York Times* (February 15, 1941).

Web Sites

Gellhorn, Martha. www.theatlantic.com/unbound/flashbks/gellhorn.htm

Miller, Lee. www.leemiller.co.uk

National Women and Media Collection. www.system.missouri.edu/whmc/womedia.htm

Phillips, Elizabeth. www.afroam.org/history/OurWar/phillips.html

Washington Press Club Foundation's oral history project. http://npc.press.org/wpforal/howto.htm

Women Come to the Front: Journalists, Photographers, and Broadcasters During World War II. www.lcweb.loc.gov/exhibits/wcf/wcf0001.html

ACKNOWLEDGMENTS

I am indebted to many people. First, of course, to all the women war correspondents who overcame seemingly insurmountable obstacles to cover the action in World War II and who later wrote about their experiences, gave interviews, and participated in the Washington Press Club Foundation's oral history project *Women in Journalism.* Then there are the writers who wrote books based on first-hand information from many of the women war correspondents. Their books were invaluable and included *Women of the World: The Great Foreign Correspondents* by Julia Edwards, *Women War Correspondents of World War II* by Lilya Wagner, and, most recently, *The Women Who Wrote the War* by Nancy Caldwell Sorel.

It was a privilege to work with the accomplished and extraordinary editor Janet Schulman. I am also indebted to assistant editor Erin Clarke, who was terrific at locating photographs, securing permissions, and tending to a myriad of details. Michelle Gengaro-Kokmen, the designer, did a wonderful job with the layout and cover design.

I also want to thank Beverly Brannan, curator, Library of Congress, Washington, D.C., who went the extra mile to track down uncataloged photographs in the *Women Come to the Front* online exhibit. Other helpful people who provided photographs include: Arabella Hayes, assistant archivist, Lee Miller Archives, East Sussex, England; Leah Lakins, archivist, the *Afro-American* Newspapers, Baltimore, Maryland; Marie Helene Gold, photograph and exhibit coordinator, Schlesinger Library, Radcliffe Institute, Harvard University, Cambridge, Massachusetts; Susan Boone, reference archivist, and Susan Barker, administrative assistant, Sophia Smith Collection, Smith College, Northampton, Massachusetts; Kurt Carroll, librarian, Newseum, Arlington, Virginia; Carolyn Davis, public service librarian, Department of Special Collections, Syracuse University Library, Syracuse, New York; Dr. Mark Brown, curator, John Hay Library, Brown University, Providence, Rhode Island; Holly Reed, archives specialist, National Archives, College Park, Maryland; Leslie Shores, assistant archivist, American Heritage Center, University of Wyoming, Laramie, Wyoming; Kristin Eshelman, photo archivist, Kansas Collection, Spencer Research Library, University of Kansas, Lawrence, Kansas; Allan Goodrich, senior archivist, John Fitzgerald Kennedy Library, Boston, Massachusetts; Lisa Hinzman, photographic reproduction business manager, State Historical Society of Wisconsin, Madison, Wisconsin; Karina Kabigting, UPI/Corbis Bettmann, New York City; Rona Tuccillo, TimePix, New York City; Elvis Brathwaite, AP/Wide World Photos, New York City; and Natasha O'Connor, Magnum Photos, New York City.

As always, I had the unwavering good cheer and support of my family, in particular those who read early versions of the manuscript, including Linda Hickson and Katrin de Haën. David Morgan Lewis-Colman helped solve a caption crisis while I was on a road trip. To everyone, I offer my heartfelt gratitude.

Picture and Newspaper Credits

Photographs on pages ix and 108 courtesy of the University of Kansas. Pages x (left), 4, 43, 49, 87, 92, and 96 © Bettmann/CORBIS. Pages x (right) and 69 courtesy of the Center for American History at the University of Texas at Austin. Pages 1 and 40 courtesy of the *Washington Post*. Page 2 courtesy of the John F. Kennedy Library. Pages 5, 7, 25, 34, 41, and 89 courtesy of the Margaret Bourke-White Estate/TimePix. Page 9 courtesy of the *New York Times*. Pages 10, 72, 75, 76, 78, 80, and 105 courtesy of the State Historical Society of Wisconsin. Pages 12, 21 (left), 21 (right), 28, 31, 44, 63 (bottom left), 63 (bottom right), 83, 97, 101, 103, and 104 courtesy of the Library of Congress. Pages 14, 16 (right), 35, and 99 courtesy of the *New York Post*. Page 15 courtesy of Carl Mydans/TimePix. Page 16 (left) courtesy of the American Heritage Center at the University of Wyoming. Page 18 courtesy of AP/Wide World Photos. Page 19 courtesy of the San Francisco History Center, the San Francisco Public Library. Page 23 courtesy of the *Baltimore Sun*. Pages 27 and 71 courtesy of the *San Francisco Chronicle*. Page 32 © P. R. Barker, courtesy of the Sophia Smith Collection, Smith College. Pages 33 and 93 courtesy of the New York Public Library. Pages 36 and 98 courtesy of the Schlesinger Library, Radcliffe Institute for Advanced Study. Page 38 © George Rodger, courtesy of Magnum Photos, Inc. Page 45 courtesy of the *St. Louis Post-Dispatch*. Page 47 courtesy of the *Los Angeles Times*. Pages 48, 51, 54, and 68 courtesy of the National Archives. Pages 52, 53, 57, 59, 60 (left), 60 (right), 85, and 95 courtesy of the Lee Miller Archives. Page 56 courtesy of the *Boston Herald*. Page 62 courtesy of the Brown University Library. Page 63 (top) courtesy of the *Afro-American* Newspapers. Page 65 courtesy of the *Atlanta Constitution*. Page 67 (left) courtesy of the Washington Press Club Foundation. Page 67 (right) courtesy of the Sophia Smith Collection, Smith College. Page 82 courtesy of the *Chicago Daily News*. Page 91 courtesy of the *Milwaukee Journal*. Page 107 courtesy of the Syracuse University Library.

AUTHOR'S NOTE

This is a work of nonfiction. Nothing in this book is made up. All the quotations come from sources listed in the bibliography.

In the course of my research, I immersed myself in newspapers and magazines that were published during World War II. I ordered photocopies of articles from librarians in St. Louis, Missouri; Cleveland, Ohio; Boston, Massachusetts; and Washington, D.C. I read articles on microfilm in libraries in New York City, Chicago, and Denver. I found Elizabeth Phillips and the *Afro-American* Newspapers on the Internet. There were also Web sites on several other women war correspondents and a Library of Congress online exhibit, *Women Come to the Front: Journalists, Photographers, and Broadcasters During World War II.*

Then there are the books—primary and secondary sources. I found my first book, *The Photographs of Margaret Bourke-White,* at an outdoor book stand in New York City in 1994. About six months later, I found my second, *Lee Miller's War: Photographer and Correspondent with the Allies in Europe 1944–45,* on a sale-book table at the Getty Museum in California. Then I discovered *The Face of War,* a collection of Martha Gellhorn's wartime articles. I was drawn to these books, although I had not yet decided to write *Where the Action Was: Women War Correspondents in World War II.* That happened several years later after I had accumulated other materials, including Dickey Chapelle's out-of-print autobiography, *What's a Woman Doing Here? (A Reporter's Report on Herself).* Reading the women war correspondents' words and seeing the women photographers' pictures was an extraordinary experience that affected me deeply and compelled me to write their true story.

I structured the book to feature the experiences of the women war correspondents, weaving their words and photographs and stories into an account of selected events that led up to World War II and that took place during the war itself. Several women, including Martha Gellhorn and Margaret Bourke-White, appear throughout the book. Others, including Dickey Chapelle, Lee Miller, Iris Carpenter, and Ann Stringer, are in one or just a few chapters. Peggy Hull, Toni Frissell, and Elizabeth Phillips are some of those who appear only in the pictures and captions. Of the more than seventy photographs in the book, all of them are either of or by the women except the images on pages 15 and 51.

This is my tenth nonfiction book about girls and women in American history. Like my other books, this one affirms the fact that throughout American history, girls and women have always been where the action was.

—Penny Colman

INDEX